WITHDRAWN

D1070058

LATER ENGLISH BROADSIDE BALLADS

LATER ENGLISH BROADSIDE BALLADS

edited by

John Holloway and Joan Black

University of Nebraska Press
Lincoln

*First published in the United States of America
by The University of Nebraska Press
Lincoln, Nebraska 68508
Printed in Great Britain*

*© John Holloway and Joan Black 1975
No part of this book may be reproduced in
any form without permission from the
publisher, except for the quotation of brief
passages in criticism*

Library of Congress Cataloging in Publication Data

*Holloway, John, comp.
Later English broadside ballads.*

*Bibliography: v, l, p.
Includes index.
1. English ballads and songs. I. Black, Joan,
joint author. II. Title.
PR1181.H59   821'.04   74-23404
ISBN 0-8032-0853-7*

Contents

Contents

Introduction

This volume is the first of several in which we intend to present something of the great wealth and variety of the English broadside ballad of the eighteenth and nineteenth centuries. Probably the 'black-letter' ballads of the sixteenth and seventeenth centuries are better known than these later ones; they have been published in large numbers in major nineteenth-century collections like (for example) the Roxburghe Ballads, the Bagford Ballads, or the Euing Collection which has only recently been published.[1] Also the earlier centuries are prominent in the only widely-known general street-ballad anthology, *The Common Muse*, edited by V. de Sola Pinto and A. E. Rodway. But the later ballads are not uninteresting by comparison with the earlier ones. They very much reflect the lively observation, gusto, love of detail and social awareness of the age of the novel; and as control of public opinion became less repressive, political satire also develops. In the eighteenth century, Irish ballads began to be composed in English and their distinctive background gave them a distinctive range of poetry; in the earlier nineteenth century the cheap printing trade expanded, and the street-ballad proliferated with it. All in all, here is an extensive, varied and important area of English literature.

The ballads in this present volume are, with only a handful of exceptions, some of them uncertain ones, from the eighteenth century; and have been reprinted from contemporary or near-contemporary broadsides in the Madden Collection. Sir Frederic Madden (1801–73), who was head of the Manuscript Department at the British Museum for many years, amassed a collection of over 25,000 printed songs and ballads; some years after his death this was acquired by the University Library, Cambridge, where it now is.

The broadside ballad of the eighteenth and nineteenth centuries is a large and intricate subject, and much work has yet to be done; some of it in specialist fields like the eighteenth-century printing trade or the history of the theatre and of popular entertainment. But the present need is in the first place to make some of the better ballads available; and the present introduction is planned to give the sort of preliminary account which may enable the texts to be read in perspective and with pleasure.

I

Pleasure, at least in a wide sense, is indeed the right idea with which to begin. The ballads were for the most part not written to give instruction or to incite to action, but to provide a moment in which listeners could enjoy verse, wit and song. 'Give ear to me a minute O / And I'll divert your minds about / Birmingham Sally O', runs one of them. The ballad called 'The Monopolizer'* (a dull, probably eighteenth-century piece we have not reprinted) has near the beginning of its text the words, '. . . it will *serve for amusement* if you will draw near'. 'Draw near' was the recurrent cry of the street-singer. Usually, his prime task was to assemble an audience, however fleeting, from those who, when they first heard his voice, had other business in hand. If he failed in that, he failed altogether. The street ballad-singer had in one sense always been no more than a special, limiting case of all those who cried their wares in the street. At the close of 'Counterfeit Halfpence'* (a ballad probably of the 1790s) are the lines:

> So now I have concluded and finished my song
> Come *buy up my ballads*, that I may be gone.

Often enough, doubtless, it was to the selling, rather than the singing, that the singer looked for such livelihood as he got.

One ballad, 'The Wandering Bard'* begins:

> I'm the wandering bard of Manchester,
> From scribbling can't refrain . . .

The vagrant nature of the ballad-singer's occupation (clearly, he was in this case also alleging himself to be the ballad-writer) comes out at once; as does the fact ('*the* wandering bard') that he is something of a distinctive and familiar figure. That this ballad was popular and served its turn—or probably did so, for there is a complication to be noted below—in a number of places, is established by two other printings which replace 'Manchester' by 'Liverpool' and 'Exeter' respectively: the song could be adapted to wherever the singer happened to be. This piece also closes with the words, 'Now buy my song . . .': once again, the performer's text suggests that sale of his wares was more to his purpose than reward for his voice. That he might also be rewarded in this respect, however, is implied at least by what is hinted at in the line:

> I came into this ale-house just to get a cup of beer.

It is clear that the ballad-singers plied their wares not in the streets only. 'The Wandering Bard', to judge by the words

*Throughout the Introduction, an asterisk by a title indicates a ballad *not* included in the present volume.

My stockings cost me fourpence
In the year of ninety-two

must be a ballad from about the year 1800.

Street-ballads were not sold by the singers alone. Thomas Hood, in one of his poems, records how the long printed slips 'danced' (in the wind, doubtless) all over a wall in Whitehall. Dickens, in *Our Mutual Friend*, published in 1863 but with its story looking back a generation earlier, describes Silas Wegg's street-stall where 'the open clothes-horse displayed a choice collection of halfpenny ballads'. Coleridge in *The Friend*[2] refers to ballads (in the time of his own childhood, the 1770s and 1780s) on the respective attractions of the various walks of life. They 'used to be sold at our village fairs, in stitched sheets, neither untitled nor undecorated, though without the superfluous costs of a separate title-page'. George Sturt in his *Journals* for as late as 1890 writes of topical songs sold from door to door in the villages 'including something . . . about the woman lately hanged at Newgate'. All these passing references show that the printed sheet-ballad was widely dispersed through London and the provinces, and in both town and country.

This is confirmed by the little snatches of self-advertisement sometimes printed on the slip-sheets: 'Printed by J. Davenport, No. 6 Little Catherine St., Strand . . . where Chaunters and Dealers etc. may be supplied with the newest articles'; 'Country orders punctually attended to'; 'Sold at 15 Long Lane, West Smithfield, Travellers and Country Dealers may be supplied'. 'Travellers' would partly have been pedlars who sold printed ballads in the rural areas (like Autolycus in *The Winter's Tale*) and whom George Sturt must have had in mind. A number of phrases here and there on individual slips make it clear that London-printed ballads were widely distributed to 'Country Dealers'.

But the provincial towns did not only sell copies from London; they printed extensively for themselves from copies circulating from London, or very often from elsewhere. Sometimes, however, ballads were not set up from printed copy at all: there are corruptions in the texts which make it clear that the setting must have been from oral recitation in the printer's office, or from the compositor's supposing that he knew the piece by heart. The broadside ballad represents a written literary tradition, but one which (and it is no surprise) comes near to an oral tradition.

Moreover, ballads were of course being composed all the time throughout the provinces, and these would have been printed locally in the first place. This happened at least from Norwich to Exeter, as far north as Newcastle or Whitehaven (in the eighteenth century, the latter town was the fifth port in the kingdom), and in Dublin, Cork, and doubtless elsewhere in Ireland. The normal practice was for the printers to market their own wares both by sale on the spot and by dispatch to other centres; printer, 'chaunter', and 'traveller' are thus three types making up a nation-wide distribution of our popular literature.

In the early nineteenth century there were developments in the printing of broadside ballads. The period was one in which new type-founts (fat-face, Egyptian and then an immense variety of ornamental founts) were being introduced almost every year. These were quickly exploited by the ballad-printers. By the 1830s many broadsheets made riotous display of 'flowers', rules and a superabundant variety of fancy types. Greater scope was also given to the printer's art by using larger sheets, with several ballads printed together in an often floridly decorative layout which was the forerunner of today's newspaper front page.

Before 1800 the 'garland' (as this form of printing was called) certainly occurred, but it seems to have been less common. The usual form in which the ballad was printed was the single or 'slip' sheet, long and narrow, and with standard 'old face' Caslon type set up much as for a single newspaper column. Apart from an occasional use of italic face (often, though, at random or quite higgledy-piggledy), there was little variety in either text or heading. Though he is in fact referring to one kind of chapbook, Coleridge's words 'neither untitled *nor undecorated*' point to the main form of ornamentation in the eighteenth-century slip-sheet—the woodcuts, employed almost invariably at the head and occasionally also at the foot of the piece.

These blocks were used again and again. Though few only that we have seen on eighteenth-century pieces must have come down from before 1700, their connection with the ballads they go with is often arbitrary and slight. Yet in one respect the woodcuts have special interest. During the eighteenth century the distinction between street-ballad 'popular' verse and more literary verse becomes so complicated as in the end quite to break down. Before 1700 it was rather more clear cut; but at least from the time of *The Beggar's Opera* (1728), and more generally as the London pleasure gardens and amusement houses developed, that ceased to be so.

In the first place, the street performer became a well-recognized stage turn for the concert room or the amusement garden. In 1793, for example, an engraving by J. Eginton from a work by H. Singleton was published with the title 'Little Bess the Ballad Singer'. Almost certainly it illustrated not a genuine street-singer, but the professional who is recorded as doing a stage ballad of that name in about 1794.

4

'Little Joe the Chimney Sweeper', a contemporary or perhaps rather later piece, is equally clearly a concert ballad (and a poor one, though we have included it for its interest in this respect). On the other hand, Rowlandson's engraving of 1800 entitled 'The vocal strains of the Ballad-singer and her family' clearly depicts a concert singer. Many of the blocks on the printed ballads also suggest that pieces printed by the street-ballad printers, in exactly the style they used for the literature of the streets in the fullest sense, probably originated as stage pieces. The block above 'The Dustman's Delight' shows a shepherdess, facing front, her arm in a characteristic stage singer's gesture, as she stands against a stagily symmetrical background. Above 'The Fish Girl', a wasp-waisted harvest girl with high, tight-laced, deeply cleft bosom and hyacinthine curls, leans on a harvest-rake before an even more stagy backdrop. Above 'The Contented Husband'*, a gentleman in elegant costume stands open-mouthed, apparently singing, before the same stagy scene. His left arm is extended in a characteristic singer's gesture, in his right hand he holds an inconspicuous tablet such as singers use for their text. The blocks with 'Belinda's Complaint' and 'Collin's Ghost' show unmistakable stage singers.

Quite possibly, some or even most of these were recognizable portraits of contemporary stage performers. But to a great extent these concert ballads appear to have circulated like the others. This is probably truer of pieces which had (as many of them indeed had) a good deal of the vernacular raciness of the popular ballad in the strict sense, than of others; and with few exceptions it is these we have chosen for the present collection.

One need not be surprised that the concert hall or theatre, as well as the street, could show strength and raciness. This is not the place to discuss the 'poetic diction' (as it is often, if misleadingly, called) of the literary poetry of the eighteenth century. But it remains true that, at least out of the context of high-style poetry, the upper classes had ready access to racy English; as they had also, if it comes to that, to the popular ballad. Sir Charles Williams was author of 'The Old Coachman'* (1742), a political ballad on the subject of Lord Carteret and his friends being stranded in their coach (the coachman was drunk), and being helped by their political opponent Lord Orford. In 1775 the same author wrote 'The Unembarrassed Countenance'*, on an occasion when Pitt, though a Minister, voted with the Opposition. Both were ballads in a popular style, probably to the traditional ballad-tune, 'A Cobbler there Was. . . ' . In 1731 Pulteney wrote 'The Honest Jury'*, on Chesterfield's celebrated acquittal on a charge of seditious libel; and in 1742 appeared 'A New Court Ballad'*, which Horace Walpole affirms was by Lord Hervey (Pope's 'Sporus').

Again, both were popular pieces, sung probably to the old tune of 'Packington's Pound'.[3]

On the other hand, the concert halls and amusement gardens of London (many of which held regular ballad-concerts) catered for all classes. It was they who gave scope to the few ballad-writers whose names occasionally appear on the slip: G. N. Reynolds, Thomas Coffey, George Savile Carey, G. A. Stevens, and of course 'Mr. Dibdin'—whether Charles or Thomas being not usually specified. Occasionally, concert tunes became well enough known and liked to be passed on from one set of words to others: several ballads were set to 'The Lamplighter', from Charles Dibdin's *The Oddities*.

Many of the popular ballads deal with characteristic ballad situations recurring in one piece after another. There are the lovers parted by the press-gang (sometimes at the instigation of irate parents); the soldier or more often sailor who returns to his true love; and the soldier, sailor or country bumpkin, come up to town, who falls dupe to the designing woman out for his money (sometimes, true enough, it is she who is outwitted). Then there is the woman disguised as a man, especially if she disguises herself so as to follow her sweetheart to the war. One such case is that of Hannah Snell, who served in disguise in the forces under the name of James Gray, and later appeared, in the 1750s, in uniform on the stage at Sadler's Wells.[4]

These typical situations shade into the more general types, in which the great variety of the popular ballad may be seen. There are pure lyrics like 'Harry Newell' or 'The Poesy of Thyme' or 'The Maiden's Choice'; marriage and cuckolding songs ('The Old Fumbler'*); rake and whoring pieces ('The Poor Whores Complaint', 'The Rakes of Stony Batter'); general social satire, often about fashion ('Belinda's Complaint'); sporting events ('The Navigator's New Victory'*, 'Scew Ball'); crime and transportation ('The Last Farewell of John Hogan', 'The Jolly Lad's Trip to Botany Bay'); cant pieces ('The Dog and Duck Rig'); historical pieces, whether like 'Admiral Benbow' or the 'Supplement to the Tombs'*; and political skits whether radical or establishment ('Wholsome Advice to the Swinish Multitude', 'British Tars Rewarded'). The street ballad covered, perhaps more so than in earlier times, the whole life of the common people.

Much of the quality of street-ballads, and indeed of the pieces generally that were printed and published alongside them, lies in the crisp and vivid economy with which the tale is told. Facts essential to the story are included, and the listener is left to infer the rest. Transitions from one character to another (self-evident when pieces are rendered by more singers than one) are taken for granted: with

6

a single singer, they have simply to be recognized in passing as the tale proceeds.

Sometimes the line of the narrative shows a shrewd awareness of how people behave in moments of emotion. Farm-hand and lecherous farmer's wife make themselves known to each other when the farmer goes off to market, but the latter

> *. . . never a word did say.*

Such idiomatic raciness is common. In 'The Bucket of Water':

> . . . She got paid *before hand* by Master Ridout
> For to fetch him a bucket full *from the next spout*

('next' means nearest). In 'The Buck's Elegy':

> *Whom should I meet but* my own dearest comrade . . .

The unobtrusive strength of such phrases is the strength of a confident, emphatic, living speech; and one sees the same thing in 'turn him away' (= dismiss him), 'or else you'll turn out' (= I'll evict you), 'out of hand', 'my cheese it is hard', in the 'New Song' between Steward and Farmer.

Yet what is racy and vernacular can easily have the merit of more than mere plainness and honesty. In fact, wit perhaps runs more freely in ordinary men's speech than it does in writers' prose:

> It was there that I saw a fair maid
> *Apparently a going astray*
> With a bunch of rushes in her hand.
> ('Bunch of Rushes O!')

—she was indeed going astray before long. Similarly in 'New Garden Fields'*,

> I am no torment young man she did say
> I am *pulling these flowers* so fresh and so gay.

At first glance, the action confirms what the girl says; on second thoughts, by no means.

> Come all ye young sailors of courage [so] bold,
> That venture for *money*, I'll cloath you with *gold*
> ('Bold Captain Avery')

shows a more verbal kind of wit. The line of thought in the ballads is constantly enlivened by touches like this, light yet crisp.

No quality of language in writing or in song will sustain itself as a mere verbal 'device'. Style which is plain and direct nourishes itself upon apprehension of experience which is plain and direct too. What matters, what is decisive, stands fair and square before the poet: and it is this which turns what would otherwise be verbal jingle into crispness and point:

> His horse it would not take the ice
> Thus he was taken in a trice.
>
> ('A Copy of Verses on William Hurt the Highwayman')

The same kind of witty presentation as showed in the line from 'Bold Captain Avery' has seized upon a neatness, a kind of dramatic structure, at the critical point in the story.

More generally: common experience is not any mere miscellany of items, and life has its trivial, and its all-important facts. The ballad poets knew what these were, and saw them steadily and whole:

> Once I had a sweetheart but now I have none
>
> ('The Bunch of Green Ribbons'*)

> When I go to bed
> She hinders me from sleeping
>
> She was my heart's delight
> I know not what befell her.
>
> ('Harry Newell')

'Dr. Dodd's Lamentation'* is in one sense an almost illiterate piece; yet for something of this same quality, it is true and moving:

> And tenderly she did me love
> But must leave her behind.
>
> And though I've wrought this sad disgrace
> My prayer is to the Lord.
>
> And though with shame my life pays dear
> The Lord may me befriend.

In art, clarity in apprehending life reaches a point where it sees life take on a pattern: one that the plain man's apprehension may not find unaided. 'The Maiden's Moan' is organized round two ironical contrasts which the maiden herself overlooks. First the incarceration she suffers, as against that which she seeks:

> Confined to my chamber, my parents think no danger

on the one hand, and on the other,

> Had I it in my power, with him I'd spend an hour
> All in some lonesome bower.

Second, there is the emptiness of her waking life ('I am never at

8

rest') against the fulfilment of her sleeping one ('As I slept in slumber
. . .'). 'The Maid and Wife' has an almost visual pattern which
embodies the emotional one. First comes the catalogue of all her fine
clothes, and then in the second part of the poem the catalogue of her
shabby ones. Right in the middle, of the catalogues as of the girl,
comes the 'maidenhead', the losing of which caused the change from
finery to rags. 'Harry Newell' matches the transformation of love by
the new name that the singer confesses, at the beginning of the poem,
love has brought to him.

In 'The Female Drummer'* comes the pattern first of a contrast
between how the words say the girl stays a maid, while the images
seem to say the reverse; and then of another reversal: once she
marries, she turns—in fact she turns from drummer to drummed:
her husband is the drummer. With beautiful human insight, moreover, the story turns on a recognition of the one person who would
betray the secret—a *girl* who falls in love with her while she is disguised. 'The Last Farewell of John Hogan' is organized a little after
the same style. The fact that, having (it seems) raped or mutilated
his victim, he himself ends up as an 'anatomy' at Surgeon's Hall,
belongs more to wit than to serious art. But here, too, the poet shows
insight: it is only after his 'harlot gay' finds she has lost his services
because he is to be transported, that (having nothing to lose by it)
she betrays the secret which brings him not to Australia but to the
gallows. Both these ballads seem to sense a deeper and decisive
causality within life's multifarious variety.

In 'Harry Newell' one may also see what it seems to be in life,
more perhaps than anything else, which gives a shape to men's
doings, and makes those doings call out for the shapeliness of art.

> She was my heart's delight,
> I know not what *befell* her.

Necessity lies beyond men's will, and it gives their life an order
they could barely give it themselves. Some street-ballads have this
sense of necessity in a simple, everyday form, rather than a tragic one;
and it works in them, lightly and sometimes almost imperceptibly,
merely as a rhythm of the most ordinary affairs of life. In 'The
Fish Girl', a ballad organized on the pattern of the four seasons, the
girl has to 'rise before day' and has her fish of course 'for to fry', while
the seasons 'draw round'. Against these hints of a necessary course
of events unobtrusively constraining the action is all the miscellany
and gaiety of the fish themselves ('my dainty fine mackerel', 'native
meltons', 'excellent thornback').

'The Country Lass', quite probably a concert piece of some kind,
presents something of the same sense of life.

I rise in the morning my labour to pursue

sings the girl. The cock crows in winter, calling her to thaw out her icy cream; in spring the lark wakes her to other tasks; in summer she must make the hay; and in harvest time mow and make safe the corn. 'So in winter or in summer we're never *taught* to grieve'. Of course there is something here of the literary and didactic. All the same, the sense is clear of how the life of men and women gains meaning through their labour; and of how in large part it is labour which brings them face to face with its realities.

The methods of dating we have adopted are those which have seemed appropriate for our kind of material. Many ballads survive from the eighteenth century in a number of printings, occasionally a large number; but systematic collation seems inappropriate, when many collections are unindexed and the material generally is little known. When several texts have been available (often enough this has not been the case) we have chosen one, and then consulted the others where they could help with doubtful readings or matters of elucidation in our chosen text. Naturally enough, the printing of these ballads was often execrable. We have silently corrected self-evident misprints, omissions and inversions, but have been chary of seeing this self-evidence too readily. For a handful of rather more conjectural readings, we have used square brackets. Where italic founts have quite clearly been used at random (a frequent practice, not without its grotesque charm) we have emended to roman; and the same in one or two cases where capitals seemed to have been used the same way. Otherwise we have left the texts as we found them, even when tinkering might have made for clarity. In the notes, we have concentrated on linguistic matters which help with elucidation or (a little doubtfully in most cases) with the date of composition. Historical notes have been kept as brief as comprehension will allow. A considerable number of the ballads which we do not attribute to a source might doubtless be so attributed in time; but to this process of investigation there would be no end, and our primary aim has been to make largely unknown material, which we think of value and interest, both available and clear. We have reproduced the head and tail blocks (if any) from the original texts used for this edition, save in a handful of cases where they were mere smudges. Once or twice we have reproduced from another ballad, when the blocks were identical and the reproduction on the copy we have used here was unusually bad. Eighteenth-century blocks show a general decline from seventeenth-century ones, but have much interest in matters of fashion and stage history, and sometimes have genuine merits as draughtsmanship.

In subsequent volumes we propose to print (whether from the Madden Collection or elsewhere) an additional selection of eighteenth-century ballads, a substantial number of nineteenth-century pieces, and also some of the Irish ballads, which probably include the finest of all, as well as, in some cases, the strangest.

We are glad to acknowledge help at various times from Dr D. S. Brewer, Mr P. Gautrey, who first drew our attention to the Madden ballads, Mr D. I. Harker, Professor L. C. Knights, Mr A. L. Lloyd and Mr Michael Mason; as also Mr R. S. Thomson, whose advice in regard to ballad melodies has been extensive and especially valuable to us. We have also had unstinted help from the University Library, Cambridge, and assistance from time to time from the British Museum Library, the St Bride's Institute Library, the Library of the English Folk Song and Dance Society, and a number of graduate and undergraduate pupils at Cambridge University. The University Librarian at Cambridge, by his advice on photographic methods of textual reproduction, has saved us much trouble throughout.

J.H.

J.T.B.

1 *The Euing Ballads*, ed. J. Holloway, Glasgow, 1971.
2 Ed. Barbara E. Rooke, 1969, vol. 1, p. 417.
3 For these pieces, see W. W. Wilkins, *Political Ballads of the Seventeenth and Eighteenth Centuries*; for the melody, 'Packington's Pound', see W. Chappell, *Old English Popular Music*, vol. 1, p. 259.
4 See W. and A. E. Wroth, *The London Pleasure Gardens of the Eighteenth Century*.

NOTE ON THE ILLUSTRATIONS

In the original printings, the illustration appears above the printed title. For convenient reference, this order has been reversed in the present edition.

The Ballads

I

Admiral Benbow

Come all you sailors bold, lend an ear,
Come all you sailors bold, lend an ear,
Tis of our Admiral's fame, brave Benbow call'd by name,
And how he fought on the main you shall hear.

Brave Benbow he set sail for to fight, for to fight,
Brave Benbow he set sail for to fight,
Brave Benbow he set sail, with a sweet and pleasent gale,
But his captains they turn'd tail, in a fright, in a fright.

Says Kirby unto Wade, I will run, I will run,
Says Kirby unto Wade, I will run,
I care not for disgrace, nor the losing of my place,
For the French I ne'er will face, nor their guns, nor their guns.

It was the Ruby and Nassau fought the French, fought the French,
It was the Ruby and the Nassau fought the French,
And there was ten in all, poor souls they fought them all,
They value them not at all, nor their noise, nor their noise.

Unfortunate it was, by chain shot, by chain shot,
Unfortunate it was, by chain shot,
Our Admiral lost his legs, and to his men he says,
Fight on, brave boys, he says, tis my lot, tis my lot.

Whilst the surgeon drest he wounds, O he cry'd, O he cry'd,
Whilst the surgeon drest his wounds, O he cry'd,
Let my cradle now in haste, on the quarter deck be plac'd,
That my enemy I may face, till I'm dead, till I'm dead.

And there brave Benbow lies, crying out, boys, crying out, boys,
And there brave Benbow lies, crying out, boys,
Let's tack about once more, we will drive them to their own shore,
We value not half a score, nor their noise, nor their noise.

John Benbow, commanding the British Fleet in a running fight with the
French off Santa Marta in the West Indies, 19–24 August 1702, had his
legs shattered by chain-shot, but continued to direct the battle, and became
something of a legendary naval hero. *cradle*, standing bedstead for a
wounded seaman (*OED*, 1803). Variant texts of this ballad appear in
Graves, *English and Scottish Ballads* (but without stanzas 4 and 7), and
Pinto and Rodway (ed.), *The Common Muse* (where the 'Nassau' appears
as the 'Noah's Ark'). At the foot of the slip-sheet from which this text has
been taken is the note:

> Printed and sold by J. Davenport, No. 6, Little Catharine-street,
> Strand, London, Where Chaunters, Dealers, etc., may be supplied
> with the newest Articles, on the most reasonable Terms.—New Copies
> printed with punctuality and dispatch.

For the melody and its background, see B. H. Bronson, *The Ballad as Song*
(1969), pp. 18, 36 ('Sam Hall's Family Tree'); and W. Chappell, *Popular
Music of the Olden Time*, p. 678.

2

The Air Balloon Fun

A New Song

You frolicksome lads and you lasses draw near,
And an air balloon ditty you quickly shall hear,
An amiable lady, as people report,
Would go a ballooning being fond of the sport.
                    Fall lara.

Fam'd Count Zambeccari form'd a balloon,
And some people say 'twas as big as the moon;
Where Cupid before his arch tricks never play'd,
By which a young lady was to be convey'd,
                    Fall lara.

We cannot but speak now in praise of the fair,
The balloon was got ready, some thousand were there,
When the lady was in that his thing would not rise,
The people did gaze on the Count with surprize.
                    Fall lara.

But as disappointments crowd on us a-pace,
The lady was forc'd to alight from her place,
Some praising her courage, whilst others they cry'd,
I am sorry, dear madam, you're depriv'd of your ride.
                    Fall lara.

The Count and brave Vernon ascended, we hear,
A beautiful prospect the sky being clear,
I'll bet five to one, had the charmer been there,
She'd have felt the effects of inflammable air.
                    Fall lara.

Near Horsham in Sussex the air balloon fell,
The wind being brisk yet they manag'd it well,
Some cordage gave way from the tube or the cawl,
Which had lik'd to have caus'd them a terrible fall.
                    Fall lara.

Full thirty five miles in one hour it run,
And just like a whirlwind the air balloon spun,
They heard such a terrible noise in the air,
They thought that Old Belzebub follow'd them there.
                    Fall lara.

But since that the Ladies all hazards will run,
This summer will bring forth some air balloon fun,
The charming young creatures so artful are grown,
They now go in search of philosophers stones.
                    Fall lara.

You lads and you lasses I'd have you prepare,
You may couple together like birds in the air,
And if you shou'd get a young daughter or son,
You sure will remember the air balloon fun.
                    Fall lara.

Count Francesco Zambeccari launched the first balloon to ascend from English ground from the Chelsea artillery-ground on 25 November 1784. The balloon landed near Petworth, Sussex, two and a half hours later. The account in the *Encyclopaedia Britannica* indicates, contrary to this ballad, that the balloon was unmanned. Cf. 'Lunardi' (no. 70). The first line of this ballad suggests that it may have been written for performance in one of the public gardens of the time. Ribald second meaning throughout.

3

Albertus The Second, or, The Curious Justice

Assist me, a Rustick, O Muse, to indite
A Story that's true, in a Manner polite;
So shall the Sage Justice attend to my Song,
A Garland that does to his Worship belong.
    Derry down, etc.

A Village there is, with a River, whose Streams
Near *Hampton*, but opposite, mix with the *Thames*;
Here lately A-float a poor Infant was found,
New-born, and suppos'd by its Mother was drown'd
    Derry down, etc.

Ah! cruel the Swain, to betray thus the Fair
To sin against Nature, when urg'd by Despair!
Or the Nymph, or the Swain, which the guiltier was?
She murder'd, 'tis true, but his Vice was the Cause.
    Derry down, etc.

This Tragedy soon reach'd the JUSTICE's Ear,
Who resolv'd, to the Bottom he'd search the Affair,
His Warrant went forth to Maid, Widow and Whore,
That strait they should come all his Worship before.
    Derry down, etc.

Obedient they went, all but one, who stood out;
She merits a Husband, for being so stout;
Record her, my Song, as a Heroine brave,
For she scorn'd to submit to a Search, like a Slave.
    Derry down, etc.

The rest, as I said, to the JUSTICE repair,
Who sits all-tremendous within his Arm'd Chair;
Some Law [. . .] before him, suppose *Nelson's Treatise*,   [?-book
And learned *Albertus*'s Book, *de Secretis*,
    Derry down, etc.

In Aid of his Sight, through an Optick he looks,
Alternately poring on each of the Books;
In one to instruct him, stands by him his Brother,
And gravely a Midwife expounds him the other.
    Derry down, etc.

At length, after all this great Pother was o'er,
He could not a Maid from a Mother explore:
Too hard it was for him (as SOLOMON said)
To find out the Way of a Man with a Maid.
    Derry down, etc.

But here stops the Muse; lest his Worship should take
The Fancy likewise in her SECRETS to rake;
And perhaps he would find, should she say any more,
Who dar'd this, her Off spring, to lay at his Door.
    Derry down, etc.

Clearly a literary stage piece, but the figure of the rustic come up to town
was widespread as a seventeenth- and eighteenth-century convention.
Albertus, Albertus Magnus, famous as an Aristotelian scholar, d. 1280.
Nelson, probably William Nelson (fl. 1720), writer of legal texts. The chorus
words indicate that the piece was sung to one of the favourite ballad-
melodies of the time (Simpson, p. 172). For many versions of the melody,
often known as 'King John and the Abbot of Canterbury', see Bronson,
vol. 1, pp. 354–61.

4

Belinda's Complaint for the Loss of her Tete

Of all the gay nymphs of the ton,
  No head like Belinda's was drest,
A tete sure as large never shone,
  With ribbons and curls of the best;
Its curls like great guns to the sight,
  And powder'd all charming in taste,
But now I have lost my delight,
  No head sure was e'er so disgrac'd:

A hat too with feathers so gay,
  Which nodded and wav'd with the wind,
Its charms to the wind did display,
  And a pad of sheep's wool stuck behind;
But feathers, and tete, and my pad,
  With ribbons all twisted around,
Are gone, and I almost am mad,
  For fear they should never be found.

Which way it could go I declare,
　　To this moment I never could guess,
Unless some live things in the hair,
　　Have thus march'd away with my dress;
Tis greasy a little you'll find,
　　By which if 'tis mine you may know,
And a smell it will sure leave behind,
　　Which some people call a ho-go.

Ye dressers all over the town,
　　To you all my grief I declare,
O find me my tete to put on,
　　Or else my poor skull must go bare;
I'll give for your pains a good price,
　　A price that is wonderous big,
You shall have all the nits and the lice,
　　Besides you shall dress my rare wig.

Satirical attacks on silly female fashion, and also on finery covering up uncleanliness, were an eighteenth-century commonplace. *Tete*, 1756; *ton*, 1769; *OED—hogo* = *haut goût*, 'a putrescent flavour, a stench'. The block printed at the head of this ballad seems fairly clearly to show a singer in an open-air stage setting. Last line doubtless ribald.

5

Birmingham Sally

A New Song

Printed by J. Davenport, No. 7, Little Catherine street, Strand, London

You pretty blooming lasses,
Give ear to me a minute O,
And I'll divert your minds about,
Birmingham Sally O.
She was fair, she was lovely O
But mam and dad so surly prov'd,
I could not wed my Sally O.

One morning to my Sally I went,
For to salute her O,
My mother she then heard it,
And vow'd she'd be my ruin O;
She cry'd is there no other
Fitting for your station O,
I'll speak, I'll speak unto your father,
He'll send you for a Sailor O.

23

O do not be so cruel,
To banish my dear Sandy O,
Do not force him from me,
He is so brisk and bonny O;
I love and I adore him,
Nothing can be said for it O,
If you banish my young laddie,
I surely shall run crazy O.

It came unto her father's ears,
He cry'd, I'll have no such doings O,
He has incurred my displeasure,
I'll banish him the nation O;
What does she mean, a saucy jade,
To be so stout and sturdy O,
A very pretty thing indeed,
So your name is Birmingham Sally O.

So all you pretty damsels,
That fancy a young laddie O,
Stick close to him you love,
And never mind your daddy O;
For Birmingham's a charming place,
There are lads and lasses plenty O,
Search city, town, and country round,
None comes up with pretty Sally O.

Many eighteenth-century ballads (e.g. 'On Board the Victory') make use of the idea that irate parents could use the press-gang to terminate unwelcome love-affairs This ballad is not literary in style, but the abrupt transitions from one 'speaker' to another suggest as a possibility that it may have been written for several singers performing together: the block shows a man and woman performing a stage duet, or out walking together.

6

The Black Cow, or, Michaelmas Morn

Last Michaelmas morning I wak'd in a fright,
I got up and went out as soon as twas light,
The morning looking both pleasant and fair,
My fancy led me towards Hornsby to steer.

Of the best geneva I then took a glass,
Then over the fields and the meadows did pass,
In the fields and meadows I took my —— [word missing.
All with an intention bird-catching to see.   What survives
is '-eg-e-'

And as I was walking by the side of a road,
There did I see some blackberries grow.
To moisten my mouth some of them I took,
So tempting and so nice they did look.

As I wander'd about I chanced to see
A girl and a cow standing under a tree,
I hasten'd up to her, and said with a sigh,
One pennyworth of milk, for I'm very dry.

The girl she answer'd me with a frown,
Ev'ry drop of my milk is spilt on the ground,
For yonder black cow that's got a white tail,
Has kick'd down my milk and bruised my pail.

She kick'd down my milk I had for to sell,
And what to do for it I cannot tell,
But if I should chance to meet with a friend,
I'd pay them again if a shilling they'd lend.

Then I pull'd out shillings by one, two, and three,
I said, my dear jewel, come hither to me,
The girl at me looked wonderful shy,
The sight of the money made her draw nigh.

A shilling I'll give you before we do part,
And for a short time you shall be my sweetheart,
Under the hedge sat Robin so stout,
The girl for a shilling gave a staunch bout,
At Ivory barn you know very well,
They've milk to spare, and some to you will sell.

This piece has much of the traditional ballad style, especially in its
pregnant and profuse imagery, but must be eighteenth-century. *geneva*,
'hollands' gin (*OED*, 1706). A handwritten note on the slip-sheet reads '42
Long Lane'—i.e. Evans. The block for this piece is almost, though not
quite, identical with that for no. 5 'Birmingham Sally' above, and it therefore seems that Evans has copied one of Davenport's blocks or *vice versa*.

7

Blarney's Rambles

Tune—The Pad

[Sold at No. 42, Long Lane]

Twas Saturday night, if I recollect right,
When first I set out from London,
I tickled a girl, her name it was Sall,
And she and her brat were both undone;
The constable wrath, he took his staff,
Thro' streets and thro' courts did me harass,
So for fear of a fray, I took my body away,
And she saddl'd her brat on the parish.

CHORUS

So young blades bold and free, take pattern by me,
I know how to persuade and to carney,
Howe'er girls may shame, they all love the game,
They love to be tickled by Blarney.

To Barnet I got, and I call'd for a pot,
The innkeeper's daughter she brought it,
I coax'd her awhile, she gave me a smile,
And we play'd at—but who would have thought it?
The father came in, and he set up a grin,
No intreaties his passion could hinder,
While he made a dead stand, I took it in hand,
And coolly dropt out of the window.

Next to St. Alban's I mov'd, and there as I rov'd,
With a girl I'd an amorous scene,
We made our abode—one side of the road,
And I gave her—you know what I mean;
Next a boarding school Miss I happen'd to kiss,
In vain the Duenna forbade it,
All the school envy'd Miss, and long'd for the bliss,
Nor was easy till all of them had it.

Thus wherever I go, the young, high or low,
The soft raptures they long to enjoy,
Tis elixir of life, the curer of strife,
And pleasure that never can cloy;
Let some, if they will, the human kind kill,
To increase 'em I'm sure I had rather,
For in twenty years hence, some of England's defence,
May look up to me as their father.

Probably an early nineteenth-century stage-piece (*girl* pronounced *gal*
seems also to be nineteenth-century). *carney*, wheedle. *set up a grin*, possibly
'tried to catch me' (see *OED*).

8

The Blind Sailor

[Sold at No. 42, Long-Lane.]
Printed in June, 1794

Come, never seem to mind it,
Nor count your fate a curse,
However sad you find it,
Yet somebody is worse;
In danger some must come off short,
Yet why should we despair,
For if bold tars are fortune's sport,
They still are fortune's care.

Why, when our vessel blew up,
A fighting that there Don,
Like squibs and crackers flew up
The crew, each mother's son;
They sunk, some rigging stopt me short,
While twirling in the air,
And thus, if tars, etc.

Young Peg of Portsmouth Common
Had like to have been my wife,
Long side of such a woman
I'd led a pretty life;
A landsman, one Jem Devenport,
She convoy'd to horn fair,
And thus, tho' tars, etc.

A splinter knock'd my nose off,
My bowsprit's gone, I cries,
Yet, well it kept their blows off,
Thank God, 'twas not my eyes;
Chance if it again sends that sort,
Let's hope I've had my share;
Thus, if bold tars, etc.

Scarce with these words I'd outed,
Glad for my eyes and limbs,
When a cartridge burst, and douted
Both my two precious glims;
Well then, they're gone, cry'd I, in short,
Yet fate my life did spare,
And thus, tho' tars, etc.

I'm blind, and I'm a cripple,
Yet cheerful I wou'd sing,
Were my disasters triple,
'Cause why, 'twas for my King;
Besides, each christian I exhort,
Pleas'd, will some pittance spare,
And thus, tho' tars are fortune's sport,
They still are fortune's care.

Probably a stage song (despite the appeal in the last verse); the sentiments
are very characteristic of Dibdin. *convoy'd to horn fair*, cuckolded. *bowsprit*,
nose (*OED*, 1961). *douted*, doused. *glims*, eyes (c. 1790).

9

The Blue Lion
Tune—Mrs. Casey

Near to a Lane, a place of fame,
    Fine fun you may rely on,
With ale as fine as any wine,
    I mean the fam'd Blue Lion;
Where Poll and Sue, with bonnets blue,
    To see each night rely on,
They'll cut a dash, and hear the flash
    Thrown off at the Blue Lion.

CHORUS

So come away, without delay,
    Where fun you may rely on,
Such songs, such gigs, such flashy rigs,
    Each night at the Blue Lion.

31

From Spitalfields, leave looms and reels,
   See Spinning Jenny come, sir,
To blade it there, with flaunting air,
   She's togg'd out very rum, sir;
From head so high her streamers fly,
   Tho' scarce a bed to lie on,
You her will see, so full of glee,
   Stuck up at the Blue Lion.

Lads of all trades, such flashy blades,
   Each night to this place going,
With natty gig, strut, look so big,
   And fix upon a blowing;
There's Powder Puff, he's shav'd enough,
   His neckcloth smart will tie on,
Lac'd waistcoat too, with stockings blue,
   The swell of the Blue Lion.

There's Scamping Ned, who without dread,
   On Finchley takes the aire, sir.
With female friends his booty spends,
   To this place they repair, sir;
When cash grows short, he must resort
   To scamp all he comes nigh on,
He cuts a swell, and rings the bell,
   For wine at the Blue Lion.

Into his room the Traps they come,
   There's no one then can bail him,
To Newgate sent, there to repent,
   His courage it doth fail him;
Without delay must garnish pay,
   The darbies too they try on,
He, with a sigh, bids a good by
   To all at the Blue Lion.

Now Newgate's bell his fate does tell,
   Alas! it is a pity,
There is not such a lad as he
   Now left in all the city;
Upon the scaffold he doth come,
   The twist they then do tie on,
The trap doth fall, adieu to all
   Flash pals of the Blue Lion.

flash, cant talk. *lads of all trades*, a specific reference to apprentices. *gigs*, jests, tricks, but in stanza 3, probably the vehicle. *blowing*, girl. *scamp*, to rob on the highway (Partridge, 1750–1840). *traps*, officers. *garnish*, money extorted from new prisoners by the gaoler (cf. *The Beggar's Opera*, Act II, sc. 7). *darbies*, handcuffs. *twist*, [hangman's] rope. *Trap* here is part of the scaffold; but the 'new drop' was not established until the later eighteenth century. Noted as '42 Long Lane' in an early hand on the original. The tune 'Mrs. Casey' is also cited for no. 119 ('Unfortunate Billy'): see also the note to no. 67 ('Landlady Casey').

10

Bob and his Landlady: or the Young Soldier's Frolick

A New Song

Upon the march it was my lot
  A billet for to share,
Unto an inn, which made me grin,
  To see my dame so fair:
My landlord he prov'd kind to me,
  And I got quarters there;
And it's true I kiss'd my landlady,
  Let that stand there,
  Let that stand there.
Tis true I kiss'd my landlady,
  Let that stand there.

Our lousy landlord blam'd me,
  For doing of this deed,
Because I did relieve his wife,
  When in the time of need:
Being a petty constable,
  For him I do not care:
It's true I kiss'd his pretty wife,
  Let that stand there.

Our orders were for Ireland,
    I did to her declare,
Which made my handsome landlady
    Begin to curse and swear,
Saying, I'll go along with BOB,
    Let BOB go e'er so far;
My BOB's the lad that kiss'd me well,
    Let that stand there.

Farewel my loving landlady,
    I must pursue the rout,
Dear BOB, says she, pray stay with me,
    Let's have the other bout:
I'll rob the cuckold of his gold,
    And thou the same shall share;
For thou'rt the man that kiss'd me well,
    Let that stand there.

Then twenty guineas in my hand,
    She lovingly did squeeze,
Dear BOB, says she, pray think on me,
    When you are on the seas:
Pray think on me, I will agree,
    With you all fates to share;
For thou'rt the man that kiss'd me well,
    Let that stand there.

The reference to Ireland possibly suggests a date in the 1790s or soon after. The guinea was withdrawn from circulation in 1813, and the last stanza therefore suggests a date prior to that. *petty*, parish. *rout*, troop.

II

Bold Captain Avery

Come all ye young sailors of courage so bold
That venture for money, I'll cloath you with gold.
Come resort unto Croney, and there you will find
A ship call'd the Fanny, shall pleasure your mind.

Bold Avery commands her, and calls her his own,
And he'll box her about, boys, before he has done,
French, Spaniards, Portugese, and Heathens likewise,
He's made a war with them 'till the day that he dies.

She's rigg'd and mann'd, and most neatly trimm'd,
She's moulded like wax work, and sails like the wind,
She has all things in order, fit for our design,
God prosper the Fanny, she's bound for the main.

Farewell to Plymouth, Catwater be d——n'd,
For once I was owner of part of this land,
But since I'm disown'd, Adieu! I will take
My person from England, my fortune to make.

I'll cross the south sea, with courage so bold,
For my men I resolve to cloath them with gold,
Five hundred and fifty brave boys of courage,
Resolv'd the first ship we meet to engage.

These Northerly climes are not fit for me,
I'll cross the tropics, that all men may see,
That I'm not afraid to let the world know,
I'll cross these seas, and to Persia will go.

I'll honour St. George, and his colours bear,
Good quarters I'll give, but no nation share: [?spare
For the world must supply me if ever I want,
I'll give them my pills when my money grows scant.

36

Lo! this is the course I intend to steer,
They that honour St. George the better shall fare:
For he that refuses shall surely soon 'spy
Strange colours on board my Fanny to fly.

Three shivers of gold, with a red flow'ry field,
Embroider'd with gold, sir, that shall be our shield.
So call you for quarter as soon as you see
Our bloody flag hoisted, this is our decree.

No quarter I'll give, nor no quarter I'll take,
There's not one man living, one glass is too late.
For we are sworn brothers, and tis my design,
I'm bound for the Indies, the gold shall be mine.

Now this is the course I intend for to steer,
My hard-hearted nation to you I declare,
I have done you no wrong, so you may me forgive,
For my sword shall maintain me as long as I live.

My commission is large, for I made it myself,
My capstan may stretch it wider by half,
'Twas dated at Croney, believe me, my friend,
In the year ninety-two, boys, unto my life's end.

Avery seized the *Charles II* at Corunna (= *Croney*) in 1694, turned pirate, and sailed to Madagascar (see the reference to crossing the tropics in stanza 6) and the Indies. *Catwater*, an inlet to the NE of Plymouth Sound. *pills*, cannon balls. *one glass*, one turn of the hour-glass (= a half-hour), the common measure of time at sea in the eighteenth century. For further discussion of this piece, see pp. 7–8. The block used is the same as that for 'The Brags of Washington' (no. 12).

The Brags of Washington

Come all you brave seamen and landsmen likewise,
That have got an inclination your fortunes to rise,
That have got an inclination to fight the proud Bostonians,
And soon we'll let you know that we are the sons of Britain.
                    Fal lal.

As for the brags of Washington, that never can be,
There is Carlton and Clinton have shewn their bravery,
There is Darby and Rodney commanders of the ocean,
And many a brave fellow is waiting for promotion.
                    Fal lal.

And if you meet a privateer, or a lofty man of war,
We never stand to wrangle, to jangle, or to jar,
We give them a broadside, and say, my lads take care O,
And keep your proper distance from an English man of war O.
                              Fal lal.

And if they will not fight us, but from us run away,
All with our heavy chain-shot we'll cut their masts away,
And if they will not yield to us, nor unto us surrender,
We'll split their ship in pieces, and to the bottom send her.
                              Fal lal.

As for the brags of Washington we care not a pin,
We will fire at his breast-works, and make him let us in,
Our bomb shells and cannons shall roar like mighty thunder,
And by our constant firing we will make them to surrender.
                              Fal lal.

And when the wars are over, if fortune saves our lives,
We will bring great store of riches to our sweethearts and our wives,
And drink a health unto the lad that has a heart to enter,
That man can never gain a prize that is afraid to venture.
                              Fal lal.

Written 1775–80. Those mentioned in stanza 2 were Commanders on the
British side in the American War of Independence. The block for this
ballad is the same as the preceding one, and shows the deck of a pirate ship.

13

The Breakfast

A New Song

As Jove, when he rises triumphant from night,
Repairs where his Hebe and nectar invites,
So joyous I spring from the gay bed of bliss,
To Jenny's arch looks, and the tea-kettle kiss.

CHORUS

Of nectar like this, of this Hebe I boast,
While she pours the sweet stream, she herself is the toast.

The stoic would feel, and the hermit would burn,
Where disabille Fanny sits over the urn,
Her youth is as rich as the liquor she sips,
The sugar less sweet than the sweet from her lips.

As the milk she infuses, she's fair and she's kind,
Yet the leaf that she draws has less strength than her mind,
Fond pleasure the charm of her bosom elates,
As the fresh moulded cream the soft crumpet enflates.

To crown the repast, she conceals not a charm,
Of ringlets disordered, of white neck and arm,
To the urn, while this iron transfuses the fire,
Bright love from her eyes shoots his darts of desire.

A charming piece, if obviously theatre-style. *crumpet* (*OED*, 1769) could not (we think) carry its modern slang overtones, but there is no doubt of the ribald possibilities of the piece as a whole. A handwritten note on the slip-sheet reads '42 Long Lane'.

14

Britannia's Lamentation
On the Devastation War

Come my sons mourn with your mother,
  At the melancholy news,
From New York and other places,
  Where Britons now do rendezvous,
Blood and slaughter still continues,
  While our foes Advantage take,
The consequence of such commotions,
  Makes Britannia's heart to ach.

See the stately Towns a burning,
  Here the shouts and dismal cry,
Mothers with their children mourning,
  While their fathers dead do lie.
Hear the roaring cannons thunder,
  See one Army run away,
The other briskly push for plunder,
  In North America.

On the infant weeps the mother,
  My tender babe my breasts are dry,
Your fathers kill'd I am starved with hunger,
  While the rest around do cry,

Once I had a pleasent table,
  Famine threatens now to come,
My house is changed into a stable,
  This my dears is now my doom.

View the camps in deep entrenchment,
  Where the fruitful garden stood,
See the ground they fought their Battles,
  Strewed with bones and stain'd with blood,
Nothing now but devastation
  Is the prospect every way.
Kind heaven stop the desolation
  In North America.

View the son pursue the father,
  Brother against brother fight,
  When they both was joined to gather,   [?together
  Beat their faces with sweet delight,
No power then could stand against us
  But in fear would run away,
Now those foes are laughing at us,
  Alas! Alas! America.

When a house is thus divided,
  It seldem does continue long,
Quarrels make us poor and weaker,
  While our foes grow rich and strong,
This is now the case of Briton,
  Oh! gracious heaven stand our friend,
And in mercy shine upon us,
  Bring these troubles to an end.

Composed in the later years of the American War of Independence (*c.*
1778); but the style is markedly archaic, as can be seen especially in the
exhortations to 'view' the horrors of war, and the conception in stanza 5 of
how civil war (here, more especially, rebellion by the son, i.e. the younger
colony) breaks up the family. The block is a crude version of that used for
no. 10 above ('Bob and his Landlady').

15

British Tars Rewarded

The tars of Old England have long toil'd in vain,
From the time of King Charles, down to this present reign,
But their Royal Master their wages doth raise,
So join, British sailors, in King George's praise.

The fleet of Lord Bridport, the terror of France,
Petition'd the throne, that their pay might advance,
Their petitions were granted, each grievance redress'd,
In the heart of each seaman great George he is bless'd.

No longer neglected, no longer forlorn,
Brave seamen will wander, dejected, our scorn,
Their petitions are granted, each grievance made known,
Soon met with redress at the foot of the throne.

Cheer, cheer British seamen, your sails now unfurl,
Against our proud foes soon defiance we'll hurl,
Our toils are rewarded, advanc'd is our pay.
Success to those seamen who gain'd us the day.

Adieu pretty Nancy of Portsmouth, adieu,
When your William is absent, I pray then be true,
To fight for our King and our country we go,
Our toils are rewarded, we'll face the proud foe.

Farewel to our children, farewel dearest wives,
We don't leave you distress'd, tho' we venture our lives,
Our pay is advanced, which you shall receive,
Then dry up each tear, girls, and cease for to grieve.

Then my boys hoist your sails, to Old England adieu,
No longer oppressed, to you we'll prove true,
You shall find that a tar is both grateful and brave,
We'll die but our King and our country we'll save.

Three cheers lads, three cheers lads, we lose sight of land,
In defence of our country we'll join heart and hand,
And when we return, boys, we'll drink, dance, and sing,
With wives, and with sweethearts, so God save the King.

Lord Bridport, second-in-command to Howe at the 'glorious first of June'
(1974), was in command of the fleet which mutinied at Spithead in 1797,
and was sympathetic to the seamen's cause. This gives a fairly exact date
for the ballad, which was perhaps meant (see the last stanza) to be sung
aboard ship, and to set the naval authorities in a sympathetic light.

16

The Bucket of Water

Tis a mighty fine thing to be sure,
It is now, without e'er a bull or a blunder,
I vow, we can sing a new song on a crafty old cow,
    That was call'd Tibby Crocket,
    Who frisk'd a man's pocket,
I don't mean of purse, watch, trinket, or locket,
But of such a droll thing, as a Bucket of Water.

This ragged old runt carry'd water about,
And she got paid before hand by Master Ridout,
For to fetch him a bucket full from the next spout,
    And so Tibby Crocket,
    That way pickt his pocket.
I don't mean of purse, watch, trinket, or locket,
But the cash that she bon'd for a Bucket of Water.

For he waited with patience till twelve for his tea,
And he then went to breakfast without his bohea,
While the price of the water she soon wash'd away
    So you see Tibby Crocket,
    Thus pickt the man's pocket,
I don't mean of purse, watch, trinket, or locket,
But of such a droll thing as a Bucket of Water.

But when Justice Old Trudge Bucket once gripes you so fast,
As she's watching your waters, I plainly forecast,
At the gallows you'll sure kick the bucket at last,
    And you'll then, Tibby Crocket,
    No more pick a pocket,
I don't mean of purse, watch, trinket, or locket,
But the thing that I mean is a Bucket of Water.

And for you, Master Ridout, since that is your name,
When you ride out or walk out beside a clear stream,
Never make duck and drake of your cash and that same,
    Since you know Tibby Crocket,
    One day pickt your pocket,
I don't mean of purse, watch, trinket, or locket,
But of such a droll thing as a bucket of water.

We do not properly understand this lively piece. The *OED* gives 1819 as
first date for '*bone*' as 'steal'; but the ballad is surely a good deal earlier.
'Kick the bucket' for die is recorded in Partridge (1) from the late eighteenth century.

17

The Buck's Elegy

As I was walking down Covent Garden,
　Listen awhile, and the truth I'll relate,
Who should I meet but my dearest comrade,
　Wrapt up in flannel, so hard was his fate.

Had I but known what his disorder was,
　Had I but known it, and took it in time,
I'd took pila cotia, all sorts of white mercury,
　But now I'm cut off in the heighth of my prime.

Doctors take away your mercury bottles,
　For I am going to draw my last breath,
And into my coffin throw handfuls of funeral fine,
　Let them all see that I die a sad death.

When I am dead wrap me up in funeral fine,
　Pinks and fine roses adorning my head,
Come all gallows whores that do mourn after me,
　Let them all follow me unto my grave.

There is Capt.——, and likewise Capt. Townsend.
　These are the men that shall hold up my pall;
Come draw up your merrymen, draw them in rank and file,
　Let them fire over me when I lay low.

Come bumble your drums, bumble them with crapes of black,
  Beat the dead march as we go along,
Come draw up your merry men, draw them in rank and file,
  Let them fire over me when I lay low.

Perhaps the implication of this moving piece is simply that the buck and his 'dearest comrade' have been promiscuous with the same women. *bumble*, one sense is 'bandage for blindfolding' (*OED*). *merry men*, companions in arms of a knight or outlaw chief (*OED*). For *pila cotia* (= *pill of cochia*, colocinth, an early remedy for venereal disease) and *white mercury*, see Reeves, *The Everlasting Circle*, p. 226. The head block used was that with no. 16, 'The Bucket of Water'. For melodies see e.g. *Journal of the English Folk Song Society*, vol. IV (1909–13), pp. 325–6; and vol. V (1915), pp. 193–4. These are for 'The Young Girl cut down in her Prime', one of several versions kindred with the above. See also R. Vaughan Williams and A. L. Lloyd, p. 108.

18

Bunch of Rushes O!

As I walked out one morning,
    It was to take some pleasant sport,
Down to a chrystal fountain,
    Where few people did resort;
It was there I saw a fair maid,
    Apparently a going astray,
With a bunch of rushes in her hand,
    That she had been gathering all that day.

Good morning to you fair maid,
    Where are you going this way so soon?
I have been gathering of green rushes,
    Kind sir, and now I am returning home,
Then fair maid come along with me,
    Down to some shady grove,
And for ever I will prove constant,
    I'll swear by all the powers above.

Then this lovely maid consented,
    And on the grass they did sit down,
It being dewy weather,
    The fair maid spread her camblet gown,
Saying, you're going to delude me, sir,
    Because that I am poor and low,
But I pray young man don't teaze me,
    Nor break my bunches of rushes O!

Now since that I have consented
    To lay these rushes down,
My mother she will chide me,
    When home to her I do return;
And if a baby I should get,
    The world on me would scoff and frown,
I shall remember gathering rushes,
    And the spreading of my camblet gown.

Rushes, gathered for thatching, were also a female symbol. Reeves, *The Everlasting Circle* (no. 48), has a variant of this song collected by G. B. Gardiner (Southampton, 1906) but lacking ll.21–8 of the text above. For melody, see F. Purslow (ed.), *Marrow Bones* (1965), p. 8.

19

Captain Barton's Distress on Board the Litchfield, being under Slavery 17 months and 14 days

Come all you brave seamen that plows on the main
Give ear to my story to true to maintain,   [?so true
Concerning the Litchfield that was cast away
On the Barbary shore by the Dawn of the day.

The 10th of november the weather being Fine,
We sailed from kingsale Five ships of the line,
With two boms and two frigates with transports also,
We was bound unto goree to fight our proud foe,

The 29th of november by dawn of the light,
We spied Land that put us in a fright,
We strove for to weather but we run quite a ground,
The seas mountain high made our sorrow abound,

Our mast we cut away our wreck for to ease,
And being exposed to the mercy of the seas.
Where one hundred and thirty poor seamen did die
Whilst we all for mercy most loudly did cry.

Two hundred and twenty of us got on shore,
No sooner we landed but strip'd by the mours   [Moors
Without any subsistance but dead hogs and sheep
That was drove on shore by the sea from the ship.

For seven days together with us did remain,
Our bodys quite naked for to increase our pain
Till some christian merchant that lives in the land,
that sent us relife by his bountiful hand

Unto our Fleet the same fate did share,
then unto morroco we all marched there,
Where they are captives in slavery to be
till old England thought proper for to set them free

When the black king we all come before
He strok'd his long beard by mahomet he swore
they are all stout and able and Fit for the hoe
Pray to my gardens pray let them go

We had cruel mors our drivers to be
By the dawn of the day at the howe we must be
Untill fore o'clock in the afternoon,
without any submison boy work was our doom

If that you offer for to strike a more,
Straightway to the king they will have you before,
Where they will basternade you till you have your fill,
If that will not do you, blood they will spill,

So now in Morrocco we shall remain,
Untill our Ambassadore cross the Main,
Where our Ransom he'll Bring and soon set us free,
And then to Gibralter we will go speedily.

So now my brave Boys to Old England were are known,
We will have Store of Liquors our Sorrow drown   [?to
We will drink a good health success never fall,
Success to the Bawd and the whores of kingsale.

Matthew Barton (1715?–95), was in command of the *Lichfield* which in 1758 was part of the squadron destined for Goree. On 28 November a heavy gale scattered the fleet off the African coast near Masagan, and the next morning some 220 survivors of the *Lichfield*'s crew of 350 reached the shore to be taken as slaves by the Emperor of Morocco. After long negotiation they were ransomed by the British government, and arrived at Gibraltar in June 1760. *bom(b)*, a small war-vessel carrying mortars, a bomb-galliot (*OED*). *were are known* (last verse), prob. 'we are boun(d)'.

20

The City Feast or, The Humours of my Lord Mayor's Show

A New Song

On a day of great triumph the Lord of the City,
He swears to do justice, so observe but my ditty,
He rides thro' the town for the rabble to shout him,
For wonderful deeds that he carries about him.
    Sing tantarara, huzza! huzza! sing tantarara, huzza!

I saw the folks run from all parts of the town,
So I trotted to gaze at his chain and his gown,
With my legs in a kennel, and up to my middle
In dirt, with my stomach as sharp as a needle.
    Sing tantarara, sad plight, sad plight, sing tantara, sad plight.

I stood in the cold clinging fast to a stump
To see the wiseacres march by in their pomp,
Like snails o'er a cabbage they all crept along,
Admir'd by their wives and huzza'd by the throng.
    Sing tantarara march on, etc.

The companies follow'd each man in his station,
To their arses in dirt, it was worth observation,
All cloathed in fur, in ancient decorum,
Like bears they advanc'd with bagpipes before 'em,
    Sing tantarara fine fun, etc.

Carry'd by the crowd from the place where I stood in,
The devil to do there was all of a sudden,
'Twas the man in armour as fierce as a lion;
Odzooks are they taylors to make cloaths of iron.
    Sing tantarara surpriz'd, etc.

A troop of codgers, O! then there came by,
In their red colour'd robes of a very deep dye,
Some staggering with drink, some hobbling with corns,
Some searching their heads, as if groping for horns.
    Sing help them along, sing tantarara along.

Then up comes a noise of untunable pipes,
With a march that would give a musician the gripes,
One of Holloway, Hampshire, or Hoggishland jigs,
Like the squeaks and the grunts of a sow and her pigs.
    Sing tantarara how droll, etc.

Their wives from the windows of every story,
See their husbands go by in the heighth of their glory,
The old cuckold he's pleas'd that his wife does behold him,
But who stands behind her I've not yet told him.
    Sing tantarara poor man, etc.

At last comes a concert of trumpets and drums,
And the mob crying out here he comes, here he comes;
I was struck with surprize, with wonder did stare,
To see servants and horses, the coach and my Lord Mayor.
    Sing tantarara fine show, etc.

The Sheriffs they follow'd him gaudy and fine,
And Aldermen's coaches good lack what a line;
But alas! it had like to have cost me a fall,
Yet I by a project got into Guildhall.
    Sing tantarara a scheme, etc.

The napkins were folded on every plate,
Into castles and boats, and the devil knows what;
Their glasses and bowls made a very fine show,
And sweetmeats like cuckolds stood all in a row.
    Sing tantarara a feast, etc.

Then all went to work with such rending and tearing,
Like a kennel of hounds on a quarter of carrion;
When down with the flesh they claw'd off the fish,
With one hand at mouth, and 'tother in dish.
    Sing tantarara stout guts, etc.

When claret and sack had roul'd freely about,
And each man was laden within and without;
The gluttons were rising, all stagger'd away,
So thus ended my frolic on the Lord Mayor's Day.

codger, from 1756 (Partridge (1)). The use of *project* for 'trick' suggests an early date.

21

The Cobler's End

A New Song

A Cobler there was, and he liv'd in a stall,
Which serv'd him for Kitchen, for Parlour, and Hall;
No coin in his pocket, no care in his pate,
No ambition had he, nor no duns at his gate.
        Derry down, down, etc.

Contented he was, and he thought himself happy,
If at night he could purchase a jug of good nappy,
O then he would wistle and sing too most sweet,
Saying, just to a hair I have made both ends to meet.

But love, the disturber of high and of low,
That shoots at the pheasant as well as the beau,   [?peasant
Shot the poor Cobler quite thorough the heart,
I wish he had shot some more ignoble part.

It was from a cellar this archer did play,
Where a buxome young damsel continually lay;
Her eyes shon so bright when she rose e'ery day,
That she shot the poor Cobler quite over the way.

Then he sang her love songs as he sat at his work,
But she was as hard as a Jew or a Turk;
Whenever he spake she'd flounce and she'd fleer,
Which put the poor Cobler quite into despair.

So he took up his awl that he had in the world,
And to make away with himself was resolv'd;
Then he pierc'd thro' the body instead of the sole
So the Cobler did die, and the bell it did toll.

The Last of the Cobler is sad to relate,
There's an End of poor Snob, but no End of his fate;
No mortal came near him, no shroud could he have
No coffin prepared, nor no care for a grave.

And now in good-will I advise as a friend,
All Coblers take warning by this Cobler's end,
Keep your hearts out of love, for you see by what's past,
That Love brings us all to an end at the last,
        Derry down, etc.

22

The Coblers Funeral

A Song being a Sequel to the Coblers End

Now the last of the Cobler is sad to relate;
There's an end of poor Snob, but no end of his fate,
No Mortal came near him, no Shroud could he have,
No Coffin prepar'd, nor no care for a Grave.
   Derry down, etc.

At length this young damsel being mov'd with compassion
And resolv'd after death to follow the fashion,
Having lain full six days till his Leather was shrunk,
She cram'd the poor Cobler into an old Trunk.
   Derry down, etc.

A tatter'd black petticoat she gave for his Pall,
'Twas supported by six crooked Coblers all,
With straps in their hands, but no cloaths to their backs,
Their mourning was so solemn, 'twas size and lamp black,
   Derry down, etc.

Six hunch back'd Gin drinkers went limping behind
Their Eyes swell'd with grief they were almost stone blind
Also linkmen, lamp black-makers, and a knife grinder,   [*sic*
As mourners mov'd after, each led a Ragg finder,
       Derry down, etc.

And when that they all were come to the ground,
They set down the old trunk, whilst the mourners stood round
Then in went his Peggs, wax, auls, shoes, soals & thread,
Whilst Gaynham the Parson most heartily pray'd.
       Derry down, etc.

Then tagg ragg and bobtail they made up the throng,
And follow'd the Corps as it mov'd a long,
Oh! had you but heard their squeeling and squealing
You'd have thought it had been the wild Irish howling.
       Derry down, etc.

Therefore in good will I advise as a friend,
Each Cobler take warning by this Coblers end,
Keep your hearts out of Love, for you hear by what's past,
That death brings us all to an end at the last.
       Derry down, etc.

The punning in the first of these two companion pieces seems early
nineteenth-century, but type and block in those printings we have seen
suggest an eighteenth-century date, as perhaps does the reference to 'the
wild Irish'. For the melody in each case, see Simpson, p. 172, and cf. p. 20
of the present volume. *snob*, a nickname for a cobbler (*OED*, 1781).
end, a length of shoemaker's thread pointed with a bristle.

23

The Cold Rainy Night or Cupid's Adventure

A New Song

In the dead of the night, when all things are at rest,
And Mortals asleep and take their ease,
Cupid knock'd at the door, she wak'd with surprise,
Saying, Who is there that calls my rest to destroy.

　Be not surpriz'd, he answer'd so mild,
For I am a little unfortunate Child,
Its a Cold Rainy Night and I'm wet to the skin,
And I've lost my way, so pray let me in.

Then up with compassion and struck up a light,
She open'd the door, and the boy appear'd in sight,
He'd wings on his shoulders, the wet from him blew
And with his bow and arrows a quiver he drew.

She stir'd up the Fire, down by her he set,
She took up a Napkin to dry up the wet;
To dry up the Wet, and keep off the cold air,
And with her hands she wrung the wet from his hair.

The cold it went out, and the warmth it gave ease,
Then touching his Bow, said, Ma'am if you please,
He said Ma'am if you please, have you experience to know,
Whether the rain has damag'd the strings of my bow.

O then his quiver and arrow he drew,
He touch'd the strings, and twang went the Bow,
So twang went the bow, in her bosom did venture,
No sting of any hornet no faster could enter.

Then off shot the arrow as blythe as a bee,
I wish you much Joy my fair one, said he;
My bow is not damag'd, nor neither my dart,
But you'll find some trouble in bearing the smart.

Probably eighteenth-century. *Have you experience to know* is a phrase
reminiscent of Irish ballads. The blocks, despite their Cupids, give no
evidence of having been cut specially for this ballad (cf. no. 29, 'The
Country Lass').

24

The Collier of Croydon

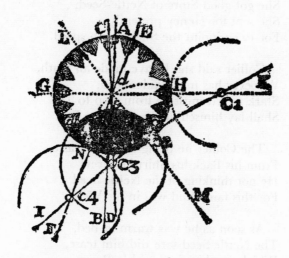

A Collier of Croydon had Coals to sell,
A wise and witty Man was he,
He would up to London ride,
To sell his coals so speedily.

As he was riding along the Road,
As he used for to do,
There did he spy a beautiful Maid,
As she appeared just in his View.

Collier, said she, is your Coals round
How do you sell them a Sack or so.
I sell them for ten, take you 'em for nine
O no says the Damsel that ne'er will do.

I'll give you eight and I'll take 'em all,
Her Beauty soon made him agree,
He them in both great and small,   [*?took* them in
For he loved this fair Maid heartily.

Half a Crown i'll give you he said,
For one Night's Lodging in your Bed
What are you so sleepy kind Sir she said,
Then of your Humour you shall be sped.

It being in the midst of Summer time,
She got good Store of Nettle-Seed,
She sent for Honey presently,
For to go 'noint the Sheets with speed.

Collier said she I have made an Oath,
Whoever has my Maidenhead,
Stark naked must be from Top to Toe,
Shall lay himself down all in my Bed.

The Collier he being in great Haste,
From his Back his Shirt he threw
He not thinking of the Nettle Seed
For this fair Maid was in his View.

As soon as he was warm in Bed,
The Nettle Seed sore did him tease,
Which put him into such a Rage,
He cry'd a Vengeance take the Fleas.

O lie you still you Collier bold,
And I'll come to you presently;
But he had enough for his Courage was cool'd,
He was so sore he could not lie.

The block would appear to be a diagram of a solar eclipse. Possibly the coal-black collier and the 'beautiful Maid' are intended by the dark moon over the sun: if so, the wit is subtler than usual.

25

Collin's Ghost

My daddy and mammy they liv'd in a cott,
They bought me a horse that would ramble and trot,
And at each market day it fell to their share,
To go to the market with eggs and such ware.

Scarce seventeen summers were over my head,
When over and round the village was spread,
There was not a lane, or a mile at the most,
But was haunted by something they said was a ghost.

My mammy she'd never once scrupled to swear,
She'd often seen ghosts and knew what they were,
So she spoke to my father, for he rul'd the roast,
To go in my stead, lest I should meet the ghost.

Being balk'd of my ride I was vex'd in my mind,
And resolv'd I was this secret to find,
I look'd out of doors and I see a clear coast,
I peep'd down the lane to discover the ghost.

Then who sould I see come sauntering along,
But Collin, the shepherd, singing a song,
He sung it so sweet as he lent on the post,
He beckoned—I went—for I knew him no ghost.

With his arms round my waist he so eagerly prest,
I thought my poor heart would have leap't out of my breast,
He kiss'd my sweet lips till as warm as a toast,
And so eagerly then, I was prest by the ghost.

Being pleas'd with my fancy, I got home with speed,
My mammy she never once miss'd me, indeed,
So instead of my supper, my ale, and my toast,
I nightly attend, well pleas'd with the ghost.

'41 Long Lane' noted in an early hand on our printing. Probably a concert piece, the block above clearly showing a concert singer, possibly a recognizable one.

26

Copy of Verses, Made upon the Unfortunate Beauty, Miss Elizabeth Taylor, now under Sentence of Death in Newgate, for robbing her Master

In Highgate as I now do tell,
One Betsey Taylor there did dwell,
Who was a beauty of renown,
But now her roses are pull'd down.

With Mr. Hooker did reside,
A young man wish'd her for his bride,
They fix'd upon the wedding day,
But all their joys are fled away.

Her brother was a wicked blade,
This poor young girl he did persuade,
To rob her master, wicked deed!
Which makes her tender heart now bleed.

Two hundred pounds in goods they stole,
Now Christ have mercy on each soul,
For they were ta'en, and cast to die,
So in the dreadful cells they lie.

When at the bar this fair maid stood,
The tears ran down just like a flood,
The roses from each cheek were fled,
She droop'd, with heart as cold as lead.

When to the bar, poor soul was brought,
For mercy on her knees she sought,
The Judge unto her then did cry,
There is no help, for you must die.

When from the bar they did her take,
With grief her heart was like to break,
Her sweetheart he was in the court,
His dearest girl for to support.

When back to prison she did go,
And they must part, O fatal woe,
The scene of grief no tongue can tell,
When she was led into the cell.

With aching heart she now does lie,
Until the day that she must die,
When drest in white from top to toe,
To meet her fate this maid will go.

So maidens now take warning all,
Reflect upon her wretched fall,
And when you hear the dread bell toll,
Fall on your knees, pray for her soul.

O! may her death atonement make,
Christ her precious soul then take,
Arm her to meet the fatal blow,
When she doth sink to shades below.

cast, condemned. Noted in handwriting on the original as '42 Long Lane'.

27

A Copy of Verses On the barbarous Murder
of Mrs. Campin, Mistress of the George Inn,
at Wanstead, on Sunday the 13th of August,
by her own Sweetheart, who afterwards
killed himself

Good Christian people give Attention,
A melancholly tale you'll hear,
And when the same I come to mention,
It sure must shock each humane ear.
A murder lately was committed,
Concerning of a little pelf;
And when the fact he'd perpetrated,
This murderer murdered himself.

At Wanstead upon Epping Forest,
Mrs. Campin of the George Inn;
Was courted by a cooper at Limehouse,
And shortly would have married been;

But a dispute between them rising,
Making Provision for her child,
Which to the cooper was displeasing,
What man could act like him so vile.

Returning in a few nights after,
His old addresses to renew;
She giving him a flat denial,
Told him the match would never do.
Of that he seem'd little affected,
And staying there till it was late,
The servants all to bed was order'd,
Resolv'd this advantage to take.

Thus being left alone together,
He soon deprived her of life;
A mortal Wound he quickly gave her
In the neck with a large knife;
And afterwards in his own belly,
He plung'd the dreadful weapon in;
Not content with the sin of murder.
Self-murder too! O horrid sin.

The wound he gave himself not mortal,
He cut his throat as people say;
As Mrs. Campin dead was lying,
He close down by her side did lay.
A shocking sight to see next morning,
In blood and gore together dead;
And what to all was more surprising,
She with her arm under his head.

How strange the devil must work in him,
To force him to a sin like this;
If Self-murder's not forgiv'n,
He's lost to hope of future bliss.
Most gracious God who reigns in heav'n,
Preserve us all both night and day;
Call on the Lord both late and early,
And for his great Protection pray.

28

A Copy of Verses on the notorious
William Hurt, who was taken near
Walthamstow; now under sentence of Death
in Newgate, for robbing John W—, Esq;
on the Highway, of his Watch and Money

All you by folly led astray,
Give ear unto my words I pray,
In the snares of Satan don't entwine,
To honesty always incline.

A highwayman of noted fame,
William Hurt it is his name,
In company with other two,
To an honest life they bid adieu.

All mounted on their stately steeds,
For Southgate then they did proceed,
They robb'd a carriage near that place,
By hue and cry were quickly trac'd.

They parted then without delay,
And Brown he took for Holloway,
A post chaise there he quickly stopt,
And all the passengers he robb'd.

The post-boy then with courage great,
A horse unharness'd they relate,
His horse run down at Islington,
And there they took this highwayman.

On the marshes leading to Walthamstow,
One the turnpike gate he did get thro',   [?delete 'the'
A hue and cry was given strait,
To stop the other at the gate.   [?him at the other

At the turnpike man he swore amain,
That he'd instantly blow out his brains,
But seeing the force so great in view,
He turn'd his horse and away he flew.

And rather than to justice yield,
He rode into a marshy field,
His loaded pistols he pull'd out,
In defiance rode the field about.

Water and ice did him surround,
The officers he did confound,
Immediate death he did declare,
To any one who him came near.

But in this life you'll plainly see,
What fate ordains it sure shall be,
His horse it would not take the ice,
Thus he was taken in a trice.

To Newgate sent, they did him try,
Both Brown and him condemn'd to die,
In shame brought to a wretched state,
See their folly but too late.

All honest ways now ever tread,
Tho' mean and low you get your bread,
Forsake bad ways you will quickly find,
A happy life and peace of mind.

29

The Country Lass

[Sold at No. 42, Long Lane.]
Printed in July, 1794

I am a brisk and bonny lass that's free from care and strife,
And sweetly does my hours pass, I love a country life,
At wake or fair I oft am there, where pleasure is to be seen,
Tho' poor, I am contented, and happy as a queen.

I rise in the morning my labour to pursue,
And with my yoke and milk pails I tread the morning dew,
My cows I milk, and there I taste the sweets that nature yields,
The lark she soars to welcome me into the flowery fields.

And when the meadows they are mown, a part I then must take,
And with the other village maids I go the hay to make,
Where friendship, love, and harmony amongst us there is seen,
The swains invite the village maids to dance upon the green.

Then in the time of harvest how cheerfully we go,
Some with their hooks and sickles, and some with scythes to mow,
And when the corn is safe from harm, we have not far to roam,
But all await to celebrate and welcome harvest home.

In winter when the cattle are fother'd with straw,
The cock doth crow to wake me my icy cream to thaw,
The western winds may whistle, and northern winds may blow
Tis health and sweet contentment the country lass doth know.

So in winter or in summer we're never taught to grieve,
In time of need each other their neighbour will relieve,
So still I think a county like all others does surpass,
I sit me down contented, a happy country lass.

Possibly a contemporary concert piece. *fother*, (north country) fodder.

30

The Country-man Out-witted: or,
The City Coquet's policy

As I walk'd forth to take the air, all in the Month of May,
I heard a Damsel talking she bonney blithe and gay,
She took me by the Hand, and she call'd me by my Name,
She said she knew my Friends, and the Place from whence I came.

I to the Tavern took her, where we did knock and call;
A Supper was provided, and costly Cheer withall;
Two Rabits there were roasted, besides other good Cheer;
Two Rabits there were roasted, and brought before my Dear.

The Supper being over, our bodies to advance,
A Fidler there was sent for, for my Love and I to dance:
Where we pass'd the time away, with Joy and much Delight:
Where we pass'd the time away, the best Part of the Night.

The Musick being over and the Fidler being gone;
No-body left within the Room, but my Love and I alone:
She took my by the Hand, and led me to her Bed
And swore that I that Night, should gain her Maidenhead.

75

We began for to be merry, and my Heart it was full glad.
But judge you all kind Gentelmen, what ill Success I had:
For she rapp'd with her Heel, with her heel against the Floor,
And up there came two swaggering Blades, a-knocking at the Door.

What do you here, said Billy, and in bed with my wife;
If you don't give an Answer, it shall cost you your Life:
While the One said to the other, forbear to d——n or curse;
For altho' we do spare his Life, we will not spare his Purse.

Full Forty good Crown, and more, out of my Purse,
Whilst the One said to the Other, indeed this will not do.
Whilst the One pull'd off my Hat, the Other took my Coat
Whilst I stood trembling there, for fear they'd cut my Throat.

A Rod she had provided of a large and mighty Length,
And on my back she laid it, with all her Might and Strength,
And when she saw the Blood, she call'd me Country Fool,
And said, it was the readiest way, my Courage for to cool.

They took off my gaudy Attire and put me on mean Array,
And turn'd me out next Morning, before the Break of Day
So a Warning will I take, and a Warning as long as I live
To all such damn'd confounded Whores, no Credit will I give.

An unusually vivid and detailed rendering of a stock situation in the
eighteenth-century ballad.

3 1

Covent Garden Ramble

Printed and sold by J. Davenport, 6, George's Court,
St. John's Gate, West Smithfield, London

One night in Covent-garden
　With pleasure I did steer,
I met a pretty fair maid,
　Taking of the air;
Her shoes were made of kerseymere,
　Her stockings they were silk.
Her shift was made of the best lawn,
　And her skin was white as milk.
　　She'd a black and rolling eye.

I took this charming creature,
　I took her to an inn,
I swore I'd ne'er forsake her,
　If that she would be mine,

I detain'd this charming creature,
  So long, she would not stay,
She sigh'd and said I am a maid,
  Pray let me go my way.

I hope you will excuse me,
  I dare not stop out late,
For if my mother she should know;
  I would not for a groat;
My father he's a preacher,
  A very holy man,
My mother she's a methodist,
  And I am a true Britain.

When I kiss'd this charming creature,
  I had my heart's desire,
This little dirty stinking slut,
  Set me all on fire,
She set me all on fire,
  Which caused me for to rue,
This little dirty stinking slut
  She's one of the wicked crew.

The present area occupied by the central London vegetable market was
laid out as a public gardens by Inigo Jones in the seventeenth century.
kerseymere, a fine woollen cloth (*OED*, 1798: a possible indication as to
date). The *groat* (approx. 4d) was not issued after 1662, but for a long time
subsequently the word was used as here. Note *methodist* also. *set me all on
fire*, infected me with pox. The block shows female fashions in headdress of
c. 1770.

3²

The Curse of Scotland

We have got no dinner, alas! what shall we do,
For we are all true Englishmen, and cannot eat burgoo,
For Monday that's a Scotchman's day, for they have a jovial feast,
Burgoo is fit for Scotchmen, but for no other beast.

If you should go to Scotland, and leave your native home,
Be sure you take with you hogs-lard, brimstone, and a currycomb,
For if you chance to catch the itch, as all the Scotchmen have,
They catch it in their cradle, and carry it to their grave.

When the pig dies of the measles then they may have roast pork,
But then they are at such a loss for the use of a knife and fork,
For they have neither knife nor fork, dish, platter, spoon nor pan,
They gnaw their meat like English dogs, and sup their broth with
  their hand.

If you should chance to catch the itch, anoint ourselves full well,
And rub it in, and scrub it in, but you must not mind the smell,
If you stink worse than an old polecat, and think you are perfum'd,
They'll think you've been at Edinburgh dance, or grand assembly
    room.

So God keep me from Scotland, and all that mangy race,
For it is a nasty, mangy, lousy, itchy, dirty place.

Probably composed not long after the Union of 1707. *burgoo*, thick oatmeal
porridge (*OED*, 1704). The block is perhaps a stage-singer of the time; the
full-bottomed wig, as shown, was going out by *c.* 1730 though not on the
stage. A pencilled note on the slip-sheet reads '42 Long Lane'.

33

The Dog and Duck Rig

[Sold at No. 42, Long Lane]

Each night at the Duck Rig and Puppy,
   What a swell by the side of your blowing,
Till she meets with a spoony that's nutty,
   Then tips you the turnips my knowing;
Sherries home with a flat to be stroaking,
   Then tips you the hint at the gig,
She will meet you with gallows good joaking,
   And boast of her bilking the prig.

You gay swindling blade or collector,
   Be call'd by your pals an attorney,
Use your daddles, dear boys, to protect her,
   And bring her home plenty of money;
You may then be call'd her fine fellow,
   And be weigh'd in the scale of each trap,
She will laugh whilst you've bit to get mellow,
   And weep when you come to the Drop.

On the high [toby-splice] flash the muzzle,
  For fear that some gallows old scout,
If you at the spell ken can hustle,
  Shou'd fix you in working a clout;
Your flamer will grow gallows haughty,
  When she's told of your scaly mistake,
She will surely turn snitch for the forty,
  That her Jack should be regular weight.

Yet sink me! but I'll undergo it,
  And all the reflects of a cell,
It is such a pleasure to know it,
  To welcome the early farewel;
Then to blind all my pals with the booty,
  She'll purchase a new gown or sacque,
Why blast me! cry they, she's a beauty,
  Who still is in mourning for Jack.

How sweet is the life of a Kiddy,
  Who swaggers a summer or two,
To be call'd by the knowing ones the Tippi,   [Tippy
  And O! my sweet blowing, that you
In a rattler will go to the scaffold,
  Whose heart you might think it would break,
Till he drops with the rest of the cattle,
  She laughs, and you see them in state.

Partridge (1) gives 1775 as the first recorded date for *rig* in the sense of 'trick' or 'dodge'. The first line of the piece, and use of 'you' throughout it, suggests that it may well have been written to be sung to an audience at the Dog and Duck Inn, St George's Fields. This became a low resort between 1775 and *c.* 1799 when it was suppressed (Wroth, pp. 273–6); and the piece is likely therefore to date from that period.

The use of 'flash language' throughout gives this ballad some distinctiveness, but on closer attention seems somewhat factitious. *blowing*, blowen, a fast woman. *spoony*, simpleton (1795). *nutty*, amorous (1821). *tips you the turnips*, 'gives you the chuck'. *sherry*, make off (1788). *flat*, dupe (1760). *stroaking*, copulating (–1785). *gig*, door (late eighteenth century). *gallows*, 'very': a cant intensive (late eighteenth century). *collector*, highwayman (late eighteenth century). *attorney*, 'a legal adviser to criminals'. *daddles*, fists (1780). . . . . *of each trap*, possibly assessed as a potential arrest by each police officer. *bit*, money. *drop*, scaffold (late eighteenth century). *high toby-*

splice, as a highwayman. *scout*, a member of the watch. *spell ken*, theatre. *fix you . . .*, arrest you while stealing a handkerchief. *scaly*, despicable(?). *snitch*, King's evidence. *kiddy*, 'a flash but minor thief' (1780). *the Tippy*, the height of fashion (*c.* 1794). *rattler*, coach.

Byron (b. 1788) writes a brief pastiche of this poem in *Don Juan*, xi. 19, refers to it in his note as 'a song which was very popular, at least in my early days', and seems to imply that he learnt it from his boxing master. Line 17 of the ballad was corrupt in our broadside text ('. . . high tobe or spice') and has been emended from the quotation in Byron's note.

34

The Dog and Shadow

Accept of a song from a heart full of loyalty,
In defence of our Commons, our Peerage, and Royalty,
On that triple base all our freedom is founded,
And we will stand forth tho' by enemies surrounded.

CHORUS.

So God save the King, and let every loyal Briton's song be,
    God save the King!

Perhaps you may think from the tune I have hit on,
I mean to sing of dogs, unbecoming a Briton,
Egad, sirs, ye nick'd it, but let me implore you,   [pron. *ye*
To lend me your patience, and listen to your story.

A dog, says old Aesop, in sun-shining weather,
Was crossing a river, with heart light as a feather,
A beef-bone in his mouth, which had plenty of good picking,
More grateful to his palate than soup, frogs, or chicken.

He gaz'd at his shadow, not knowing it was his own, sir,
But thought it was a dog with a similar bone, sir,
To seize it rapidly he plung'd down his head, sir,
But dog, meat, and bone, was immediately fled, sir.

At length he began to curse his hard fate, sir,
And repented his rash folly when it was too late, sir,
At length he quite starv'd reach'd the opposite shore, sir,
And heaven only knows whether ever he eat more, sir.

Such, sirs, is my story, and now for application,
This dog in the fable is our happy nation.
The beef bone in his mouth is our glorious Constitution,
But the shadow that he saw was the French Revolution.

So Britons beware lest by Frenchmen betray'd, sir,
You let go the substance to grasp at the shade, sir,
While we feel ourselves blest let us still persevere, sir,
Except from delusion, we have nothing to fear, sir.

Now I'll dismiss the dog, sir, he has done his duty,
I have found another simile, I am certain it will suit you,
Our State is a man of war, with three masts and a jury,
Our anchor Magna Charta, and a strong one I assure you.

Our crew are all well, may no pain ever come near us,
We have got a stout ship, a wise pilot for to steer us,
Here's Billy Pitt at the helm, Charley Fox to keep watch, sir,
The devil must be in it sure if any harm we can catch, sir.

Composed in the 1790s, this ballad applies Aesop's fable to the contemporary political situation. *nick*, to guess rightly (*OED*). *You* would be
pronounced *ye* throughout, for rhyme.

35

The Dustman's Delight, or
Who paid for hobb'ling the Dust Cart

Come, come brother dustmen and listen awhile,
I'll give you a ditty will make you to smile,
It's of a rum codger, who thought himself wise,
Who met with a blank, boy, instead of a prize.

You must know with my cart I went out 'tother day
And I called for dust,—for I live by that way,
When this pretty fellow, so nice and so smart,
In the green yard he hobbled my horse and my cart.

Soon as to my master this thing was made known,
The horse and the cart from the green-yard came home;
My master, for teaching two-penny worth of sense,
An action against him he then did commence.

The trial came on at Guildhall, you shal hear,
And the thing it was proved so plain and so clear,
He'd acted unlawful, beyond all dispute,
And was cast for ten pounds, besides all cost or suit.

This was nuts for us dustmen, you all must agree,
Because now our trade is laid open and free,
The queer cull was done rumly and touch'd for his bit,
Ten pounds a great price for two-penny worth of wit.

Now I go and cry dust O, so bold and so smart,
None offers to meddle with me or my cart,
I suppose for their pocket they have some regard,
Or at least they remember the pretty green yard.

I fear neither scavenger now nor his man,
But dust I will cry, and get dust where I can;
It is an employment that's honest and just,
For you know I must want if I can't get the dust.

For as they do make it we take it away,
Or else it a week or a fortnight might lay,
Till the tubs do run over, this fact it is clear,
And when they fetch it, want a full pot of beer.

But we are the men that go every day,
And with pleasure we catch it to carry away,
It brings in the pence for to get us a crust,
For as we eat and drink we must down with the dust.

It's by dust we live now all people does know,
And in a short time all to dust we must go,
High and low, rich and poor, dust must be all our fate,
And the dust of the poor mix'd with those that were great.

green yard, the pound. hobble, to take into custody, 'nab'. nuts, a gratifying
present (Vaux). bit, money. There is a pun throughout, but especially in
the closing stanzas, on the colloquial sense of dust, money.

36

The English Rover

Printed and sold by J. Davenport, 6, George's Court,
St. John's Lane, West Smithfield

I am an English rover just come from London town,
My sport I'll not give over but ramble up and down,
When'er I meet a pretty girl that's blooming, blithe and gay
I'l make her know more than a maid before I go away.

At Brentford I was a swaggering blade sometimes a jolly tar.
The lasses oftimes on me gaz'd with eyes like shining stars,
Among the saucy ladies there I rambled night and day,
And left them all well satisfied before I went away.

At Windsor I was a soldier bold, none could me surpass,
And loyal to my King and prince, and every pretty lass;
At Wycomb town a miller good, and ground their flour fine,
The girls did all me applaud, and swore I was divine.

At Aylesbury a lace-merchant, and carried my lace box,
And oft times I my lace have sold to trim their Holland smocks;
At Oxford town a joiner good, and when I came away,
In tears the lasses round me stood, and begg'd of me to stay.

A button maker at Birmingham myself I next did call,
In which I soon was notic'd well among those lasses all,
My mettle good, their moulds true, not given for to run,
In nine months time they sigh'd and cry'd by him I was undone.

In Coventry a weaver next, my shuttle ran most free,
Their openings true, their bottoms good, I wove there merrily;
The Warwickshire young lasses all others do excel,
They are kind and free in each degree, as I the truth do tell.

The next I was a cooper, in that I took delight,
And when I came to Derby their hoops I cork'd up tight;
At Nottingham a shoe-maker as many well do know,
The lasses say I stitch'd them well from heel unto the toe.

And when I came to Leicester, a stocking maker by trade,
Then by the buxom girls counted a merry blade,
And oft times hose so fine I wove for many a pretty maid
And for to garter up the same I never was afraid.

At Northampton town a butcher, the truth I will reveal,
The lasses were so kind they from rust kept my steel;
At Wellingboro' a pedler, thus I ramble here and there,
And when I came unto St. Neot's I dealt in maiden's ware.

At Cambridge a stay-maker next I was by my trade,
And oft times there I lac'd the stays of many a pretty maid,
Till their handsome shapes and slender waists they could no longer
     show,
Their aprons and petticoats too short for them did grow.

At Bedford a stone-mason, there call'd a roving blade,
And with rule, level, plumb, and gauge, my stones careful I laid,
At Hitchin a hair-dresser, the truth I will declare,
My chief delight was day and night in dressing ladies hair.

At Hartford and Ware a blacksmith, they doctor did me call
My cordial sweet I gratis give unto both great and small,
When maids troubl'd me with love-sick pains, my bit of skill I
     try'd,
I prick'd 'em in the merry-vein and left 'em well satisfied.

Now I mean to leave off roving and take to me a wife,
Prove kind unto my loving spouse and lead an honest life,
With my bottle and my friend my social hours pass,
Drink a health to the king, queen, and every pretty lass.

Probably eighteenth-century. The words 'ramble' and 'rover' frequently
had overtones of gaiety and amorous escapade; though this is not recorded
in Partridge (1). For the *double-entendre* in *lace*, cf. 'The Flashy Lace-
Makers' (no. 42).

89

37

The Fainthearted Lover or,
The Hero Rewarded

[Sold by J. Evans, No. 41 Long-lane]

Near to St. James's there liv'd a lady,
   She was beautiful and fair,
The fairest beauty in London city,
   And worth five thousand pounds a year.

This lady she was resolved,
   That no man her husband should be,
Except it was some man of honour,
   All in the wars, by land or sea.

There was two 'squires, two loving brothers,
   That came this fair lady for to woo,
With a noble resolution,
   This young lady to pursue,

One of them had a Captain's commission,
   All under the honour of Colonel Car;
The other was a bold Lieutenant,
   On board the Tyger man of war.

O then replied the fair young lady,
   I can but be one man's bride,
So come to me to-morrow morning,
   And this matter I will decide.

So then went home these two young brothers,
    Not thinking of their fatal doom,
While she lay musing on her pillow,
    Till the morning it did come.

This lady she a maxim thought on,
    And resolved was it to try;
To see which of them was the true lover,
    And who for her sake dangers defy.

She then bid her coachman to get ready,
    And away unto the tower drove she,
It was to spend one single hour,
    The lions and the tygers for to see.

But the lion and tyger so loud roaring,
    That it put this lady in a swoon,
And for the space of half and hour,
    She lay speechless on the ground.

But when she found herself recover'd,
    Into the den she threw her fan,
Saying, which of you that wou'd win the lady,
    Must go and fetch out my fan again.

O then bespoke the faint-hearted Captain,
    Madam, your offers I don't approve,
For in the den there is much danger,
    So I will not venture my life for love.

O then replied the bold Lieutenant,
    His voice it was both loud and high,
Saying, Madam, here's that man of honour,
    That will fetch out your fan, or die.

Then into the den the Lieutenant enter'd,
    Where the lions look'd both fierce and grim;
He seemed not for to be daunted,
    But looked as grim at them again

Now when they saw his blood was loyal,
    Down at his feet, O then, fell they,
And he stooped her fan to get,
    And then he brought it safe away.

When she found her true love coming,
  And no hurt unto him was done;
Into his arms then she came running,
  Crying, my dear, take the prize you've won.

Then bespoke the faint hearted Captain,
  Like a man disturb'd in mind,
Saying, to some shades I'll wander,
  Where no mortal shall me find.

The royal menagerie was in the Tower of London until removed to Regent's Park in 1884. The ballad may be seventeenth-century. For melodies see *Journal of the English Folk-Song Society*, vol. V (1915), p. 114 ('The Lion's Den') and p. 258 ('The Bold Lieutenant').

38

The Fair Maid's desire to learn her A B C

I am a sailor of no trade,
Long time I courted a pretty maid,
And if I can't her favour win,
I'll away to sea, away to sea I'll go again.

I went unto my Love's chamber door,
Where often times I had been before
My Love she arose and let me in,
And away to bed, and away to bed she went again.

I turned down the holand sheets,
To see her beauty both fine and neat
And a little below there did I spy
Two pillars of, two pillars of white ivory.

Love shall I go, Love shall I stay,
Love shall I go some other way.
She sigh'd and sobb'd and thus she said,
Why was I born, why was I born to die a maid.

Is there never a young man will me show,
Some Letters of my criss-cross row
That I may know as well as he,
Some Letters of, some Letters of my A B C.

I put my pen into her hand,
I bid her use it at her command,
She knew full well where it was to go;
So soon she learn't, so soon she learn't her **criss-cross row.**

criss-cross row, alphabet (= Christ-cross-row, from the cross in front of the
alphabet in horn-books. *OED*, 1563). This ballad may be old, but the first
stanza suggests eighteenth-century.

94

39

The Female Press Gang or, a true and particular Account of Seven young Women, that prest Fourteen Taylors in one Night, in London

It was in London town as we do understand,
Seven lasses they took a brisk frolic in hand,
And as I protest they were in sailor's dress,
Not far from Cheapside they resolved to press
    Fourteen Taylors.

Then Nancy she ty'd her sword by her side,
Resolved she was for to be the guide,
This young female crew, Kate, Bridget, and Sue,
And she that went first was Lieutenant Prue,
    To press Taylors.

These girls by consent, their minds fully bent,
Unto the house of call at St. James's they went,
But there in the street a poor taylor did meet,
They prest him, and he fell down at their feet,
    I'm a taylor.

I tell you, says, he, I ne'er was at sea,
So pray you kind gentlemen to let be free,   [me
And pity my tears, I've been fifty years,
And never us'd weapon but bodkin and shears,
    I'm a taylor.

Without any regard unto the white yard,
Where as a poor taylor was labouring hard,
Upon the shopboard Nancy drew out her sword,
And said, you must King George your service afford,
    Tho' a taylor.

The taylor did shake, nay quiver and quake,
At length with a trembling voice he did speak,
Whilst tears down did run I'm surely undone,
For, alas! I don't know the right end of a gun,
    I'm a taylor.

But nevertheless said bouncing Bess,
You must come along, we've a warrant to press,
And we'll have no excuse, so lay by your goose,
Such nimble young fellows are fit for our use,
    Tho' a taylor.

Then unto Round Court they went by report,
Where seven taylors were making of sport,
Their hearts void of fear, but when they came there
The maids caught them napping as Moss caught his mare,
    Seven taylors.

They at first did resist, but Joan with her fist,
She thumpt them about till the taylors all pist,
And then in a rage the rest did engage,
And brought them away unto Bridwell or cage,
    Seven taylors.

Then to Tower-lane with all might and main,
These petticoat press-masters hurry'd again,
For to press where they knew both Morgan and Hugh,
A couple belong'd to the cross-legg'd crew,
    And Welsh taylors.

Then morgan he rail'd, cot splutter hur nails,
Hur is a master taylor, tho' pred up in Wales,
So pray cease your strife, for hur has a young wife,
Besides hur was never once kill'd in hur life,
    Hur's a taylor.

But right or wrong, they all tast it along,   [?haste
Till at length they did meet two more in the throng
Then said surly Jen, you must go serve the King,
These lasses they prest and brought them all in,
    Fourteen taylors.

house of call, 'the usual lodging Place of Journey-men Tailors' (*Partridge* (1)).
shopboard, raised platform on which tailors sat to work. *goose*, a tailor's
smoothing-iron. *Round Court*, off the Strand, London. *as Moss caught his
mare*, proverbial (*ODEP*, p. 856). The block shows female hair-styles of the
1770s.

40

The Fish Girl

A New Song

[Sold at No. 42, Long Lane]

My name's pretty Poll, near Thames street I dwell,
By the salesmen at Billingsgate I am known mighty well,
When I flash my new basket as the spring it abounds,
I cry my nice herrings, I sell my live sprats a penny a plate full
    all around.

I have dainty fine makarel next of course for to cry,
And the choicest of whitings for those that will buy,
And as the warm season of spring it abounds,
I cry my nice flounders at sixpence a dozen all round.

I have my charming fine plaice next of course for to cry,
And my dainty live soals for those that will buy,
And as the warm season of summer abounds,
I cry my nice maids at sixpence a couple all round.

Now St. James's day begins to draw on,
I flash my shallow at the gate every morn,
I cry my native melton's three a penny as the season comes round,
Till I cry my fine eels at fourpence per pound.

I have dainty fine skait next of course for to cry,
And my excellent thornback for those that will buy,
And as the warm season of summer abounds,
I cry my fine lobsters at two a shilling all round.

I have my charming fine turbot of course for to cry,
And my dainty fine dabs for those that will buy,
And as the warm season of autumn draws round,
I cry my nice salmon at a shilling per pound.

I rise before day, to the gate I repair,
And the choicest of fish my basket shall bear,
And as the warm season of autumn abounds,
I cry my fine museles at twopence a measure all round.

maids, fish, probably of various kinds. See *OED*, and stanza 3. *flash my shallow*, probably simply, display my barrow (*OED*, 1859). But 'do the shallow' was also a cant phrase for 'capitalizing on rags and semi-nudity' (c.19; cf. *Partridge* (1)). Presumably eighteenth century, this piece in part follows the 'round-of-the-seasons' pattern which was still a well-established literary convention. Presumably a concert-piece: the block shows what looks like a theatrical girl-harvester, with hay-rake, in an appropriately stagy setting.

41

The Fishes Lamentation

A New Song

In came the Herring, the King of the sea,
I think it high time our anchor to weigh.

    For it's hazy weather, blowing weather,
    When the wind blows it's stormy weather.

Then in came the Salmon as red as the sun,
He went between decks and fired a gun.

Then in came the Oyster with his sharp shell,
Crying, if you want a pilot, I'll pilot you well.

Then in came the Flounder with his wry mouth,
He went to the helm and steer'd to the South.

Then in came the Shark with his sharp teeth,
Let go the clue-gallants, hawl in the main sheet.

Then in came the Dolphin with his crooked beak,
Pull in the main-sheet, let go the main-tack.

Then in came the Cod with his chuckle head,
He went to the main-chains, and sounded the lead.

Then in came the Suck-pin so near the ground,
Pray Mr. Cod do you mind the wind.

Then in came the Whiting with her glowing eyes,
Take in the clue-gallants, let go the main-ties.

Then in came the Sprat, the least of them all,
He stept between deck, and cry'd, Hold boys all.

Then in came the Mackarel with his sly look,
Pray Mr. Herring do you want a cook?

Then in came the Guard-fish with his long snout,
He stept between decks, and turned about.

Then in came the Smelt, with his sweet smell,
All hands go to dinner, and I'll ring the bell.

Then in came the Crabb with his crooked claws,
I'll ne'er go to sea with such lubbers as these.

Then in came the Lobster, with his black cloak,
All hands go to sleep, and I'll go to smoak.

Its general style and rhythm is that of a sea-shanty for raising the anchor
(cf. stanza 1). *suck-pin*, possibly the 'remora'. This ballad has recently been
recorded by Mr R. S. Thomson, sung by Mr Harry Cox of Catfield,
Norfolk.

42

The Flashy Lace Makers

J. Pitts No. 14 Great Saint Andrew Street, Seven Dials

Northamptonshire, Bedfordshire, Buckenham too,
Are most of them lace-makers we know it is true,
Most of them lace-makers in every town,
None of these fine lasses shall e'er be run down.

As for these lace-makers it is their delight,
To twingle their fingers from morning till night,
They work with their pillow bobbins and pins,
And when your lace is done girls you may take it in

When trade it is shining they are all alive,
These flashy lace-makers O how they do thrive;
With fine lace on their caps a straw bonnet they'll wear,
And a bunch of blue ribbons to tie up their hair.

In come the lace buyers among all the rest,
They are all fine tradesmen they are neatly dressed,
They are as fine tradesmen as any in town,
These flashy lace-buyers shall ne'er be run down.

Round goes the lace-buyers in every town,
To see if there's any good lace to be found;
There's plenty of lace so you need not to fear,
Its so much a yard and you'll find it not dear.

There is Bedford and Buckingham Ailsbury too,
There is Leighton-buzzard we know it is true;
It is Leighton-buzzard in Buckinghamshire.
Who are all flashy lace-makers throughout the year.

So now to conclude and finish these lines,
These flashy lace-makers they are very kind,
They are very kind I'll make it to appear,
Thro' Bedford, Northampton and Buckenhamshire.

Cf. no. 36, stanza four.

43

The Flying Highwayman

Come all ye bold and swaggering Blades,
  That go in search of plunder,
With Pistols cock'd and courage bold,
  Have Voices loud as thunder.
Young MORGAN was a flashy blade
  No youth had better courage,
Much gold he got on the highway,
  That made him daily flourish.
Grand Bagnios was his lodging then,
  Among the flashy Lasses;
Soon he became a Gentleman,
  And left off driving Asses.
I scorn poor people for to rob,
  I thought it so my duty;
But when I met the rich and gay,
  On them I made my Booty.
Stand and deliver was the word,
  We must have no denial;
But alas, poor Morgan chang'd his note,
  And soon was brought to trial.
I robb'd for gold and silver bright,
  For to maintain my Misses,
And we saluted when we met,
  With most melodious kisses.

After sweet meat comes sour sauce,
    Which brought me to repentance,
For now at last I'm try'd and cast,
    And going to receive my sentence.
Up Hounslow Heath and Putney too,
    I oft made my approaches;
Like lightening I and my horse did fly,
    When I heard the sound of Coaches:
When first of all I was call'd up,
    In order for my trial,
With my beaver hat and surtout coat,
    I stood a bold denial.
I stood as bold as John of Gaunt,
    All in my rich attire;
I ne'er seem'd daunted in the least,
    Which made the court admire.
From Newgate to St. Giles's pound,
    Me and my Moll was carted;
But when we came to the gallows tree,
    Me and my Moll were parted:
So I took leave of all my friends,
    Likewise my flashy Blowen;
But now at last I'm try'd and cast,
    Out of the world I'm going.
I thought I heard the people say
    As I rode through the city,
That such a clever Youth as I,
    To die it was a pity:
I thought I heard such cries as those,
    Which set my tears a flowing;
But now allas, I'm try'd and cast,
    And out of the world I'm going.
I'm the Captain of the gang,
    All in a low condition;
But now I'm going to be hang'd,
    I'll throw up my commission.
So why should I refuse to die,
    Now here or ever after;
The Captain he must lead the way,
    His men must follow after:
The King was pleased to pardon me,
    And on me took compassion,
And freed me from the gallows tree,
    All in my low condition.

44

The Fortunate Scotchman

A New Song

Sawney, sawney, wether away,
A word or two I prithee now stay,
How came you so bonny and gay,
And went a begging the t'other day
    Bonny Scot witness can,
    England has made you a Gentleman.

The blue Bonnet when thou cam'st hither,
Scarce would keep out Wind or Weather;
But now it is turn'd to the beaver and feather
Thy bonnet is blown the de'el knows whither.

The shirt thou wore on thy back,
Was made of the webb of a coarse hop-sack,
Now tis turn'd to holland so fine,
Bought with brave English coin.

The Band and Cuffs thou used to wear,
Were scarce washed three times a year,
But now its turn'd to cambrick clear,
Deck'd with laces up to the ear.

They waistcoat and dublet were but thin
Where many a Louse has harboured in,
But now it is turn'd to scarlet red,
With silver and golden lace all spread.

Thy gloves were made of the threaden stitch,
Kept on your hands to hide the itch,
Now they're to kid leather i'm told,
Stich'd up with silver and gold.

Thy stockings made of an ordinary blue,
Scarce worth Sixpence when they were new
Now they are turn'd to the scarlet hose,
With silken garters down to the shoes.

Thy shoes when thou came from plough,
Was made of the hide of an old Scotch cow
Now they are turn'd to Spanish Leather,
Silver buckles all together.

The sword you wore was a black blade,
With a basket hilt with iron made,
But now a long rapier hangs by your side,
To huffing does the bonny Scot ride.
　　Bonny Scot, etc.

Probably composed shortly after the Union of 1707, though the elegant
rococo block suggests a later date for this printing.

45

Ground Ivy

Printed and Sold at 21, East Smithfield

Last April morn as forth I walk'd,
I roved I no not where,
I heard a voice so loud and sweet,
I could not but go there,
I could not etc.

Her Garment was mean,
Her tatter'd gown,
Upon her shoulder hung,
With blooming cheeks,
And eyes cast down,
And as she walk'd she sung,
    Ground Ivy.

Come here my pretty Girl, says I,
And tell me your name,
All in your basket, I will buy,
Come sell to me the same,
Come sell etc.

I gave her all that was in my power,
So blight she tript away,   [blithe?
I gave her all that was in my power,
I never shall forget the happy hour,
I saw her cross the way,
    Ground Ivy.

Where should I hear in lane or street,
Her voice so loud and sweet,
Where should etc.
I long my bloom ey'd girl to meet,
And hear her cry again,
    Ground Ivy.

Ground ivy was sold as a purge, but ivy generally was known as a female
symbol (see Reeves, *The Everlasting Circle*, p. 243).

46

The Highwayman outwitted by a Farmer's Daughter

At Berry there lived a Farmer
  Whose daughter to did go,   [?market
Not fearing that they could harm her,
  So often she'd to and fro.   [?gone

One day it fell out among many
  A Thief met her on the Highway,
He was dressed in Troopers apparel,
  And he caus'd this maid to stand.

Several hard blows he gave her,
  A Pistol he clapt to her breast
Your cloath and your money deliver,
  Or else you shall die I protest.

He stript first, this maiden quite naked
  And gave her the bridle to hold
And there she stood shivering and shaking,
  Just ready to perish with cold.

From stirrup to saddle she mounted
  Crying out to the Highway man

As soon as my coin Sir you've counted,
　　Then follow me strait if you can.

The rogue he starts up in a hurry
　　He run, he puffed and he blow'd
He run but he ne'er could come nigh her
　　Saying damsel I'll give you your cloaths.

No matter for I am contented,
　　Cries she to the Highway man,
And now you have got all my money,
　　You may catch me sir, if you can.

Thro' woods and green fields she passed
　　To Places she knew very well,
And left him a parcel of Farthings
　　The sum of five shillings to tell.

Her Father was so much surprized,
　　Being seven or eight of the clock,
For to see his own dearest daughter,
　　Come riding, all stript in her smock.

O daughter what has been the matter,
　　That made you to tarry so long
Dear father some thing has befel me
　　Or else I'd been sooner at home.

He took the Portmanteau from behind her
　　And opened it on the ground
And there he took out gold silver　　　　　　　　[?and
　　Amounting to five hundred pounds.

O Daughter here is five hundred pounds,
　　And I'll give you five hundred more,
And I think that's a very good portion,
　　To keep the Wolfe away from the door.

Possibly seventeenth-century. The block is unclear, but may show a
butcher's shop. *trooper* is first used in 1640 (*OED*). *Berry*, possibly Bury St
Edmunds. For the melody, see F. Kidson and A. Moffat, *A Garland of
English Folk Songs*, p. 14, and C. J. Sharp, *Folk Songs from Somerset*, 1905,
series II, p. 50 and note.

47

The Horned Miller

Near Cannon Mill there liv'd a miller,
Who lately came by a purse of silver,
How it befel I will plainly tell,
None in this town can it excel,
  O the poor horned miller O.

The miller's wife, a wanton jade,
Would frolic with another blade,
And whilst the miller watch'd his mill,
The spark the miller's place did fill,
  Which griev'd the poor honest miller.

This young man he had been about,
Amongst some customers no doubt,
Some money his accounts to pay,
And about the time of Whit Sunday.
  O the poor miller.

The miller he came home to his wife,
Whom he adored as his life,
Being loth to wake her out of her sleep,
In at the window he did creep.
  O the kind miller.

But the other spark was in the bed,
Which made the miller's wife afraid,
And being waked out of her sleep,
So bitterly began to weep.
    This grieved the poor miller.

He said, my dear, what is the matter?
I'm almost dead, I'm not much better,
I am of the cholic sadly sick,
But a dram of gin may ease it.
    O the poor miller.

He said, there is brandy in the house,
But she said, that is of no use,
My life if you regard now as one pin,
Run to the town and fetch some gin.
    O the kind loving miller.

But the miller he had doft his cloaths,
To seek his breeches strait he goes,
He got the spark's, and put them on,
Not knowing but they were his own.
    So it is, O the poor miller.

Then straight he ran to the sign of the Swan,
Crying, get up, and fetch me a dram,
Of the best gin that can be had,
My wife is of a cholic bad.
    O the poor miller.

He search'd his purse to pay for the dram,
Where plenty of money therein he found,
With a few bank notes therein besides,
I am enchanted, the miller he cries.
    O the poor miller.

How came I by this, he did say,
When he espied a watch key,
I've got a watch, all is not right,
Some man has lain with my wife this night,
    O the poor miller.

He thought of this, and he ran home,
And gave his wife a hearty dram,
Now since that I have been away,
Has any one been here I pray?
   O the poor miller.

O no, since you went to the mill,
No one has been here but your own self,
A young man was here this afternoon,
But you was here, and saw him gone,
   O the poor gallows miller.

Certainly you lie, my dear,
Or else how came these breeches here?
They are the fellow's breeches I do know.
So after him you strumpet go.
   O the poor horned miller.

gallows, in this intensive use (last verse but one) is late eighteenth-century (*Partridge* (1)). Cf. no. 33. Probably a provincial ballad.

48

Humming Bub

Dear mother I am transported
To think of those brave comrades,
They say we shall all be courted,
Kind widows as well as maids;
O this is joyful news, and
We'll stick up our houses with holly,
We'll broach a tub of humming bub,
For those that come with a rub a dub dub,
Dear mother they'll make us jolly.

Dear mother to seem mounted
Twould tickle your heart with joy,
By me they shall all be counted
Heroical sons of Troy;
They shall kiss us whenever they please.
And we'll stick up our houses with holly,
      We'll broach, etc.

These lads are the pride of Britain,
They love us, and well they may,
Dear mother it is but fitting
We should be as kind as they;
Our conduits shall run with wine,
And we'll stick up our houses with holly,
    We'll broach, etc.

I'll dress me as fine as a lady
Against they come to town,
My ribbons are all got ready.
A furbelow scarf and gown:
To welcome these warlike sons home,
We'll stick up our houses with holly,
    We'll broach, etc.

They are lusty, stout, and brawny,
They are neither too plump nor fat,
They say they are somewhat tawny,
But they are never the worse for that;
They shall kiss us whenever they please,
And we'll stick up our houses with holly,
    We'll broach, etc.

Those bustling sons of thunder,
When they're returning back,
I know they'll be for plunder,
Virginity goes to rack;
They shall kiss us whenever they please,
And we'll stick up our houses with holly,
    We'll broach, etc.

The title and the word *furbelow* date this piece as late seventeenth-century
or (more probable) eighteenth-century. *kind* (1.4), clearly carries its older,
sexual sense, and there are other *doubles entendres* in the piece: holly is a
male symbol.

49

The Humours of London

When I to London first came in,
How I began to gape and stare
The cries they kick'd up such a din,
Fresh lobsters, dust, and wooden ware;
A damsel lovely and black ey'd,
Tript thro' the streets and sweetly cry'd,
Buy my live sprats! buy my live sprats!
A youth on t'other side the way,
With coarser lungs did echoing say,
Buy my live sprats!

Still shriller cry'd the chimney sweep,
The fruit'ress fair bawl'd round and sound,
The Jew would down the area peep,
To look for custom under ground;
The bag he o'er his shoulder flung,
And to the sootman sweetly sung,
Cloaths to see—cloaths—

Round and sound—sweep!
Young soot did cry in accent true,
The barrow lady and the Jew,
Round and sound—cloaths.

A noise at every turn you find,
Ground ivey, rabbits, skins to sell,
Great news from France, and knives to grind,
Mats, muffins, milk and mackarel;
And when these motley noises die,
In various tones the watchmen cry,
By the clock—twelve—past twelve o'clock;
Then home to bed the shopmen creep,
And all the night are kept from sleep,
With past—humph—o'clock.

ground ivey: used as a purge. *muffin, OED*, 1703. *great news from Fiance* just
possibly suggests a date in the 1790s. *fruit'ress*, this form is first recorded in
OED in 1713.

50

The Humours of Rag Fair

Last week in Lent I came to town,
Having a leizure hour,
I came to see their Majesty's crown,
And the Lions in the Tower,
Loosing my way, I chanced to stray,
'Mong a lane full of second hand tailors,
I was struck with surprise, at the noise and the cries,
O! hundred second-hand taylors.

Do you want e'er coat,   [?a coat
Or a waistcoat young man.
To dress in this good Easter,
Here's breeches, fellow them if you can,
You may have them for a teaster,
A Plad Jacket, for a barber's man,
A fustian frock for a baker,
Left off clothes for Spitalfields beaus,
And black for an undertaker,

Stockings for young women so neat,
With holes above the quarter,
With clocks of white of red and blue,
All flourished to the garter,
Knit hose for Men and boys,
Silk for those that strut,
You may have them whole,
With their own sole,
Or neatly darned and footed.

Come customers buy my shoes,
Not a pin the worse for wearing,
I bought them a bargain of a maid,
Of a woman that goes a chairing
A groat a pair, search all the fair,
And try if you can match them,
The shops are so nice, they'll have their own price
Although they darn and patch them,

All smoaking hot a groat a pound
My sweet and plain plumb pudding,
The flower was the best in the Market found
And all the ingredients good in,
I makes it sweet, and gives good weight,
My pound is sixteen ounces
But bye the bye and he tells you a lie
Although he brags and bounces.

In watchouse cage I next did spy,
Strolling black-ey'd Susan
Who only took a guinea or two
From a taylor that had to loose them,
The impudent w—— when the justice before,
Said in her examination,
That the money in ful she had,
For to please his inclination.

'Tis here and there you'll find,
A stall set up by young beginners,
The houses are rented all by publicans and sinners,
Sure here is the Alderman's beer,
And a charming good fire,
I'll make you a pot of the best gin hot,
What more can a young man desire,

Some was smoaking and some at cards
And some with chaps a dealing.
Some was devote, and some blackguard
For all people have their failings,
So then I paid my score
And came out of my Meditation.

Rag Fair was the cheap clothes market in Rosemary Lane (later known as Royal Mint Street) close to the Tower of London. For the Royal Menagerie in the Tower, cf. no. 37, 'The Fainthearted Lover'. *teaster*, tester, sixpence. *quarter*, the side of the foot. *clock*, an ornamental silk thread pattern worked on the side of a stocking. The word *watch* (*-h*)*ouse* probably indicates a date before 1829, when the new police were introduced, and *chairing* in the sense char(e)ing is recorded in *OED* from 1732. The last two stanzas are defective.

5¹

The Indifferent Lover

Why should Young Women love Men so,
When Young Men will never give way
To love the Women again sir,
They will Love them for little, not long,
They will do them no right, nor take no wrong
I prithee Love leave off this flattering tongue,
    For I cannot nor will not love fondly.

Fie on your wheedling Speeches,
How many have you bewitch'd!
You will marry with any
So they have but Money,
Tho' they are as ugly as Witches.
I for my part will never do so,
If he is not handsome, for me he may go,
Surrender I do not care what you do.
    For, etc.

Then sheer your Sheep and go fold them,
For no more I will behold them:
First to the Forest, and then to the Plain,
And there for to seek for a jolly young Swain,
And so to return to my true Love again.
     For, etc.

As I sat under a Myrtle
I thought I was sure of a Turtle:
But there I did find it went with the Wind
Of every side of the Circle: [?On
And I for my part will never do so,
For if he's not handsome, for me he may go:
Surrender, I do not care what you can do.
     For, etc.

Clearly a theatre or concert song, date uncertain.

52

The Irish Beau
or Five Hundred Pound Cuckold

I travel'd from Paris to Amsterdam,
From thence I came to Old England,
And in my travels wherever [I] go,
My heart it delights in my Irish Beau.

As I was walking along Cheapside,
I met an Old Connock that wanted a guide,
Forty bright guineas I would give to know,
Come shew me the way to my Irish Beau.

As I was walking along Skinner Row,
Who should I meet but my Irish Beau,
His kisses were sweeter than any I know
The blessings go with my Irish Beau.

An Irishman's pocket it stands where it should
When one pocket's empty the other stands good
An English Cuckold wherever he goes
Is not to compare with my Irish Beau.

Lo here's a good health round let it pass
Let every british girl toss off her glass
And drink confusion to a scotchman's toe
And my blessing go with you my Irish Beau.

As for the bold sasnack I care not a stroaw,
Nor any poor devil that takeeth his part
I'll make them to labour in spite of their nose
And spend all their mony on Irish Beaus

No there's the consumption, the fits of the mother,
And the phthisicky cough the women do smother,
But wat's distress'd from the top to the toe,
The infallible cure is my Irish Beau.

The remarkable tail-block is printed upside-down on the original slip-sheet, perhaps to conceal its lack of connection with the ballad. *sasnack*, Sassenach, English. *mother*, hysteria.

53

The Irish Disapointment

Once I lov'd Lady a Lady,
   From top to toe;
But I was blockhead a blockhead
   And durst not tell her so
Could I but tell her, tell her,
   How I Languish and die
Could I but tell her,
   What a blockhead was I?

   She is very pretty
She is a little genteel
   But she is so witty so witty
The more I am bound to feel
   Could I but tell her, etc.

She is very merry
She is a little Coput   [?coquette
 Her Lips red as a chery
Her Eyes black as Jet
 Could I but tell her, etc.

 First I would ogle ogle
Then I'd squeeze her hand
 And then I would kiss her
'Till she could not with stand
 Could I but tell her tell her,
How I languish and die,
 Could I but tell her tell her
What a blockhead was I?

The block shows apothecary's equipment.

54

The Irish Lovers

Now the winter is past,
And the summer comes at last,
   And the birds sing on every tree,
The hearts of those are glad,
Whilst I am very sad,
   Since my true love is absent from me.

My father he is great,
With a plentiful estate,
   He has robb'd me of him I adore;
How cou'd he so cruel be,
To force my love from me,
   And I fear I shall see him no more.

I'll put on a coat of black,
And a fringe about my neck,
   My rings on my fingers I'll wear;
Straightway I will repair
To the Corough of Kildare,
   And tis there of my love I shall hear.

A livery I shall wear,
And I'll comb back my hair,
 I will dress in my velvet so green;
And this I'll undertake,
For my true lover's sake,
 He rides on the Corough of Kildare.

With patience I did wait,
Till he ran for the plate,
 Thinking young Jopson to see;   [?Johnson
But fortune prov'd unkind,
He has alter'd his mind,
 And he's gone from the lowlands from me.

I would not think it strange,
The wide world for to range,
 So I could but obtain my delight;
So here in Cupid's chain
I'm obliged to remain,
 And in tears I will spend the night.

My love is like the sun,
In the firmament doth run,
 That always proves constant and true;
But yours is like the moon,
That goes wandering up and down,
 And every month is new.

Farewel my joy and heart,
Since you and I must part,
 You're the fairest that ever I did see;
I never did design
To alter my mind,
 Altho' you're below my degree.

'Johnson' for 'Jopson' is suggested by the apparent link between this
ballad and 'The Lamenting Maid' (no. 66).

55

The Irish Mans Ramble

A New Song

When forth in my Ramble intending to gamble,
To an ale house I Rambled most freely,
I set with the Toppers and Drunk of full bumpers,
Till I became fudled most realey.

The Drawer did say the Reckoning come Pay,
For that is the best Play most truely,
Or else I will strip you, and heartily whip you,
And out of Door's kick you most sure Sir.

The landlady with a frown said the money lay down
Or your Cloths I will have for the Score Sir,
Your Coat Briches and Hatt your Shirt and Cravat,
I will have from your back most sure Sir.

Zouns says the Clown the Stairs kick him Down,
Till wiser he growd this alarmed,
Like a Stag from a gun through the Streets I did run,
My Carkas and bum was well warmed.

The brats of the Town with pudel and stone,
Belabourd my bones severely,
The Dogs and the Hounds my body surrounds,
Thus I pay'd for my Jaunt most dear Sir.

There was Teag with a Shovel and Bryun with a ladle
And Dermot with a wattle persued me,
And old Mother Trimble and Joan with the spindle,
And Nora the bich sore abused me.

Old Couckold Roger as gray as a badger,
Close followed after to Shoot me,
And Nora my miss that I youst for to kiss,
She would galop and trot to come to me.

This is a rambler and also a gambler,
A knave or a blockhead so fited
To see London facion the best in the nation,
My Policy there they out-witted.

But at last by my Soul my dear Joy to condole,
My misfortunes I met with a Ladey
That got me a login that Night with-out Dogin
The Prince of all stalions most greasy.

Topper, a 'top' person (*OED*, 1709).

56

The Irishman's Ramble To London

I'll stay no more in Dublin,
  To live upon potatoe fare,
But I'll go up to London,
  Arrah! Pat, won't you come, my dear?

CHORUS

Arrah! come, come away,
  My Irish blade,
Arrah! come, come away,
  Och! your fortune will soon be made.

Now the Ladies of London
  They are so very kind,
Whenever they get a poor
  Honest Teague to their mind.

As for your person tis comely,
  Both strait and tall,
To handle a shelalah,
  G——'s blood and ouns! he can't at all.

If all things should fail you,
　And nothing at all prevail,
Take the straps on your shoulder,
　And carry the milking pail.

If of all things I've told you,
　There's nothing at all will do,
Take a stick in your fist,
　Stand a pimp at some bagnio door.

But curse upon that New Drop,
　Tis fatal to Irishmen,
Whenever they handle the pops,
　Or the forging pen.

CHORUS

I'll not go away, I'll not go away,
I'll not go away, my Irish blade,
For fear of the police men.

The *Drop* was first used in hanging in 1760, but was often called 'new' for some time after that (Partridge (1) gives 'ca. 1780–1900'). Reference in the last line to 'the police men' suggests a date after 1830. *teague*, nickname for an Irishman. *pops*, pistols. This piece perhaps suggests a date for the preceding ballad only a short time before it.

57

Jack Oakum in the Suds

Tune—The Anacreontic Song

Ye lovers of grog now attend to my lay,
For strange is the news which to you I'll unfold,
Tis of an old seaman who dy'd t' other day,
Who'd long fought for England, with Rodney the bold;
Tis said, he did cry, if by fighting I die,
For preferment in shades I'll immediately try,
But in drinking success to his country so dear,
Poor Jack by chance ended his earthly career.

Jack Oakum being come to the regions below,
Spy'd Old Charon advancing to ferry him o'er,
He cry'd, bear a hand mate, now with you I'll go.
Says Charon, you ought to have been here before:
For I would be bound, were these regions search'd round,
That none near so wicked as you would be found,
The tar in a passion reply'd, you old dog,
I should not have come yet but I drank too much grog.

Old Charon look'd sternly, and thus he reply'd,
You must now be more civil since you are come here,
I judg'd at first sight you were drunk when you dy'd,
But you'll drink no more grog now your soul for to cheer,
And now, d'ye see, you must pay me my fee,
Or else you shall ne'er be row'd over by me;
Jack jumpt into the boat, and cry'd, dam'me I'll go,
So the sculls took from Charon, and over did row.

The news to great Pluto directly was told,
Who, seiz'd with confusion at what he had heard, said,
This true British hero will ne'er be controul'd,
He'll contend for some privilege tho' he is dead;
Then since he's of worth, let him take Charon's birth,   [berth
His employment will be the same then as on earth,
And for more satisfaction, go tell the young dog,
That his fare shall be changed from silver to grog.

in the suds, in a difficulty, and also 'fuddled', 'drunk' (*OED*, 1765–80). The
piece is reminiscent of Dibdin. Admiral Rodney's reputation was made
c. 1760–82.

58

Jack of the Green

It was in the month of May, when flowers they were seen,
I saw a bonny lass with Jack upon the Green,
O how they hugg'd and kist, he call'd her his delight,
And told her, if she pleas'd, he would lie with her all night.

Fie young man, said she, your words do me affright,
To think that you should crave my maidenhead to-night,
I'd not for all the world with any man be seen,
My mammy she would say, we danc'd Jack on the Green.

He said, my joy, my only dear, I'll give you guineas two,
To grant me my request, all night to lie with you,
I will young man, said she, you creep behind the screen,
When my mammy is gone to bed, we'll dance Jack on the Green.

O then this couple parted, rejoicing she went home,
To think what sport she'd have, with her own dearest John,
She kept her mammy in talk, Jack creeps behind the screen,
When her mamma was gone to bed, they danc'd Jack on the Green.

This couple fell to work, thinking they were not seen,
Whilst she learn'd these few steps, with Jack upon the Green,
Her mamma got out of bed, and by Jack was not seen,
And with an old besom's head she beat Jack off the Green.

Then Jack began to frown at feeling of the stick,
The cunning jade lay down, pretending to be sick,
Her mamma call'd her whore and sorry dirty quean,
For learning those few steps with Jack upon the Green.

Her mamma she laid on, she brake the besom's tail,
Then to get out of doors young Jack he did prevail,
He made a solemn vow he'd never more be seen
Along with a bonny lass, to dance Jack upon the Green.

William Hone, *The Every-Day Book*, 1826–7, writes of 'formerly, a pleasant character dressed out with ribands and flowers, figured at village May-games under the name Jack-o'-the-Green . . . [who] always carried a long walking stick with floral wreaths'. l.20, *Partridge* (1) records associations between *green* and what he calls 'the female pudend', but only from *c.* 1850 on; this ballad must be much earlier.

59

Jack Tar's Drunken Frolic in Wapping

Jack Tar from a cruize, and had ta'en a rich prize,
Came rolling down Wapping, D—— limbs and eyes,
Ran foul of a frigate snug rigg'd, tight, and trim,
First turning his quid, nods his head with a grin.

Jack thought his broadside would bring madam to,
Then talk'd about boarding, but all would not do,
He shew'd her his purse, said, dear jewel behold,
Don't refuse to engage me, my freight it is gold.

The sight of his guineas soon alter'd her tale,
She said, I'll be pilot, so let us make sail.
They put about ship, and soon they made port,
And came to an anchor in the bay of Plough Court.

The bawd was an ugly fat lump of a thing,
And two or three times in the pillory had been,
She welcom'd them in, and unto him said,
Use her tender, dear boy, for my daughter's a maid.

Jack being safe moor'd with his miss on his knee,
Thought none was so knowing and jovial as he,
The liquor came freely, he push'd round the grog,
And wish'd that our fleet might our enemies flog.

The influence of liquor got into his crown,
And being too heavy he fell to the ground,
They strait took his purse which contained his store,
And put him to bed with a dead blackamoor.

He snored till daylight, as I have been told,
Then turning to kiss her, he found she was cold,
On viewing his charmer he rose up in a fright,
And swore he'd been kissing the devil all night.

He jumpt out of bed, and soon put on his cloaths,
In a hurry straightway to his messmates he goes,
He told them the story, they laugh'd at the fun,
And said, d——me! Jack, why the old one was done.

His shipmates they jeer'd him, and said it was queer,
That for one night's lodging he should pay so dear,
Jack laugh'd at his frolic as do many more,
When they think how he cuddl'd a dead blackamoor.

A hand-written note on the slip-sheet reads '42 Long Lane'.

138

60

Jarvis the Coachman's Happy Deliverance from the Gibbet

My name it is Jarvis well known,
A coachman I've been for some years,
To drive up and down in the town,
Without any dangers or fears;
Till some gentlemen wanting a coach,
Gentlemen seeming to be,
   But, O had I known their design,
   The devil should have drove them for me.

They gave me ten shillings in hand,
I said for the same I would stay
Until their return home at night,
To Fulham I drove them straightway,
Where we had fowls of the best,
Methought we liv'd wond'rous free,
   But had I known, etc.

We staid till eleven at night,
And then we came rattling home,
At Chelsea I was in a fright
There I began to know my doom,
They made me drive out of the road,
Where one hung in chains you may see,
   But had I known, etc.

And when we came up to the gibbet,
They made me drive under it strait,
And then swore that up to the top
I should immediately get,
And saw the old gentleman down,
For there he no longer should be,
   But had I known, etc.

The post was full of nails drove,
I told them I could not get up,
Then one of the said gentlemen
From his pockets pull'd out a rope,
And ti'd it round my waist,
Then drew me to the top of the tree,
   But had I known, etc.

There I was hung up in a fright,
None by me but a man in chains,
I call'd out for help in the night,
But all my calling was in vain;
But when the daylight appear'd,
A gardener's wife I espy'd,
I begg'd of her to lend me an ear,
O the devil's a coming, she cry'd.
   But had I known, etc.

At length some brickmakers came by,
I begg'd of them to cut the rope,
My voice made the brickmakers fly,
They swore that the man in chains spoke;
Till at last a bold butcher came by,
Who gave ear to my pitiful moan,
Said, What, was you hang'd without law,
So poor Jarvis the coachman got down.
   But had I known, etc.

Jervis, Jarvis is a traditional name for a coachman. The last offender to be
hanged in chains after execution ('gibbeted') died in 1832.

61

The Jealous Husband well Fitted

Printed by J. Davenport, 6, George's Court, Clerkenwell

A Hosier liv'd in Leicester, as I have heard many tell,
He had a handsome witty wife, that lov'd him full well,
But he was touch'd with jealousy, as often you shall hear,
Which caus'd his handsome witty wife for to shed many a tear.

Each night he'd go a drinking and roving up and down,
And often it was midnight before he came home.
And when he came home he'd curse and call her wh——,
And threaten every word to turn her out of door.

On day above the rest, he in a jealous pet,   [One
Began to curse and call her names, and she began to fret,
At length a scheme came in her head, thought she I'll try the same,
Perhaps my conjuration his jealousy may tame.

The hosier, then, as usual, at night a drinking went,
And she to try her fancy it was her full intent,
A hairy jacket provides, with cloven shoes we find,
With two large horns upon her head, and a long tail behind.

A chimney sweeper lived near, and straight to him she went,
And told to him her fancy, and what she did propose,
She says to him, you have two hearty boys as any of the kind,
And with their help I don't fear but we can change his mind.

She and the two sweeps went home, as it is said,
She drest herself just devil like, and so she went to bed,
The one she plac'd behind the door, for to let him in,
The other she plac'd by the fire, for to burn his skin.

So presently he did come home as drunk as any owl,
Began to curse and call her names, and speak words very foul,
Saying, you wh—— get out of bed, and bring to me a light,
Straightway the sweeps came crawling in, which did him sore
    affright.

This put the jealous husband into a great surprise,
With that they did some gunpowder let off in his eyes
His wife a hairy jacket had, with cloven shoes we find,
With two long horns upon her head, laid hold of him behind.

O spare me Mr. Devil, O spare me now I pray,
And every fault that I have done I'll mend another day,
O spare me Mr. Devil, and you little devils all,
For if ever I am jealous of my wife, then you may on me call.

Well if you'll promise me a good husband to be,
And kind unto your loving wife, and use her tenderly,
My little devils I'll take off, and bid you farewel,
But if you're jealous of your wife, you shall go to my dark cell.

She laid her hairy jacket by, and of it took great care,
The sweeps they kept the secret close, her husband ne'er did hear,
But if any thing did happen they were to come again,
But he proves a good husband, and saves them all their pains.

62

The Jolly Bacchanal, or
The Bottle the Best Companion

When first to my Mistress I made my address
I told her my passion was grown to excess,
My suit she accepted but soon as the Lass
Knew how Much I valued my Bottle and Glass,
She often reprov'd me and told me, 'twas plain
Unless I left Drinking my Courtship was vain;
So now I'm resolved my pretence to decline,
Let her go to the Devil to the Devil e'er I'll forsake wine.

She tells me with Clarret she cannot agree
And she thinks of a hogshead when e'er she sees me;
That I smell like a beast and therefore must I
Resolve to forsake her or Clarret deny;

Shall I leave my dear Bottle that was always my friend,
And I hope will Continue so to my Life's end;
Shall I leave it for her 'tis a very hard task;
Let her go to the Devil to the Devil bring the other Flask.

Had she tax'd me with Gaming and bid me forbear
'Tis a Thousand to one but I'd lent her an Ear;
Had she found out my Cloe up three pair of stairs
I had left her and gone to St. James's to Prayer;
Had bid me read homily three times a day   [?Had she
She perhaps had been humour'd with little to say;
But of Night to deny me my flask of dear red,
Let her go to the Devil to the Devil in an Empty Hogshead.

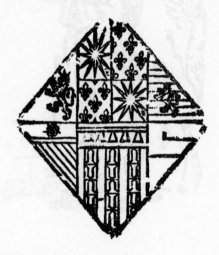

An old block, perhaps mid-seventeenth-century.

63

The Jolly Lad's Trip to Botany Bay

Come come my jolly lads, for we must away
Bound down in irons to Botany Bay,
Tis no use to weep nor to complain,
For perhaps we may see Old England again.

CHORUS

So come, come away, for I can no longer stay,
Let us hope we may meet with a far better day.

Altho' we are bound to a foreign clime,
There is many of us young lads just in our prime,
Who by wisdom we ought to have been better taught,
For wisdom's never good without it is dear bought.

Now many a pretty lass in Botany may be seen,
Who knows but she might be an Indian Queen,
Deck'd out in diamonds see the British fair,
A fig for transportation little do we care.

Now when to Botany they do us bring,
The first thing we do is to chuse us a King,
Tis no use to laugh, nor to make fun,
For who knows but it may be the noted Barrington.

Fare you well, my pretty girls, I'll bid you all adieu,
For it may be a long time before I do see you,
So fill up the glass, and drink it off I pray,
Success to the poor lads that's bound to Botany Bay.

Botany Bay, an inlet five miles south of the present city of Sydney, was used as a convict settlement from 1788 when the first expedition, of 736 convicts in all, included 188 women prisoners. This ballad must date from just after 1790, when George Barrington was transported. Originally a noted pickpocket, he was released in 1792 and later became superintendent of convicts. For some time he held a false reputation as a writer on Australian subjects, since publishers used his name in advertisements for several works. (See J. A. Ferguson, *Bibliography of Australia*, vol. 1, Sydney, 1941, pp. 13–17.)

64

The Jolly Postboy

O ye riders far and near give attention to my song,
The chaise-driving trade's the best under the sun,
The sun shines so bright without any fail,
And we are the lads that get oceans of ale.

There's the hart on the forest stands in the dale,
There's spirits and good liquor sold, beer, cider, and ale,
Tis so very fine, so clear and so good,
You may call and drink a bottle with bold Robin Hood.

There are six good horses kept at this place,
And two bonny lads to drive a great pace,
For nine-pence a mile day and night you may fly
O'er hills and o'er dales, till fair Nottingham you spy.

These horses are fed on the best corn and hay,
And good litter to lay on both night and day,
They are kept so clean from the head to the feet.
Such good accommodation you seldom do meet.

When we return with our empty chaise,
We meet a pretty girl, she may ride at her ease,
With a little persuasion up she doth get
And he soon after, and down by her doth sit.

Your person my dear I should like to enjoy,
To have ride for ride you can't me deny,
By a little persuasion he did on her prevail,
And he pull'd up her petticoats and her smock tail.

The joys of my heart we've both play'd our part,
Such jolly lads as you have fairly won my heart.
So now my dear I must away,
For my time is expired and I can no longer stay.

There is Anthony and Jack are not to be beat,
By driving the chaise, or smack of the whip,
When they have got their own heart's delight,
O then turn their backs, and so good night.

When we come to an inn down by her we sit,
Where she gives us a shilling to drink her health,
Saying my dear your name I like to know,
It is Robin in the Rushes, you may call me so.

So now to conclude and end my song,
Over hedges and ditches till we see Nottingham,
When we come to an inn there we drink our fill,
Here's a health to Robinhood, Little John, and Will.

Printed in London, but probably of local Nottinghamshire origin. The
tail-block is that printed with no. 77—commonly used by Evans.

65

The Lace Merchant Taken in by the Farmer

Sold at No. 15, Long-lane, west Smithfield

I'll tell you of a farmer that was going to pay his rent
All for to pay his landlord it was his full intent
His wife she thought he had been gone, but t'was a great mistake,
For he was in the closet set some writings for to make.
Then came a smart lace merchant in, she treated him with wine
And said my husband is from home, to love I do incline,
And I wish he never may return, such compliments she made,
So took him to a private room where bed and pillow made.
The farmer hearing what was said, his anger rose apace,
Then in the kitchen he did go where he saw a box of lace,
He took it soon and emptied it, and in same he found
Diamond rings, lace and bills, worth seven hundred pounds;
The farmer goes into the town, as cunning as a fox,
And there he got a bastard child, so he put in the box,
Then took his neighbours home with him, all for to see the fun,
So craftily he put the box into the same place again:
Then with his boots and spurs on into the room he goes,
And with a whip in hand he threw down the clothes;
Then he began to whip them, and follow'd out his blows,
The smart they could no longer bear, so they run without their
    clothes.
Not thinking of a child the laceman took his box,

And ran home like a madman, while the blood ran down his
    locks: [?hocks
When his wife saw him naked, she fell into a fit.
She thought by a gang of thieves he had been robbed and stripped.
She pitied him most deplorably and did bewail his case,
It's well you sav'd the box my dear, with the diamond rings and
    lace.
She had no sooner spoke this, when the child began to cry;
Which made the matter ten times worse, they swore most bitterly,
The merchant is forced to keep the child, which grieves him to the
    life,
A thousand times he curst the day he kissed the farmer's wife.
For horning of the farmer he paid a 1000 pounds,
Nor ever after durst he come upon the farmer's grounds.

Another ballad, 'The Flashy Lace Makers' (no. 42) probably nineteenth-century, also suggests that the word 'lace' may have had ribald overtones; but Partridge does not record this.

66

The Lamenting Maid

The yellow leaves do fly from the trees so high,
Upon the ground I see they do fall,
The man that I adore has lately left the shore,
Which grieves my poor heart worse than all.

The winter's gone and past, and the summer's come at last,
And the small birds are on every tree,
The hearts of those are glad while mine is very sad,
Since my true love is absent from me.

Farewel my dearest dear until another year,
Till the sweet spring I hope I shall see,
The linnet and the thrush will charm in the bush,
And the cuckow will charm in the tree.

I'll put on my cap and black fringe all around my neck,
Rings on my fingers then I will wear,
Straitway I will repair to the county of Kildare,
And there I shall have tidings of him.

My father he was great in a plentiful estate,
He has forc'd my true love from me,
How cruel could he be to force my love to sea,
I'm afraid I shall never see him more.

The livery I will wear and comb down my hair,
Then I dress in my velvet so green,
Straitway will repair to the county of Kildare,
Tis there I shall have tidings of him.

With patience I did wait till they'd run for the plate.
And thinking young Johnson for to see,
Fortune prov'd unkind to this sweetheart of mine,
Now he's gone to the lowlands from me.

Farewel my joy and heart, since you and I must part,
You are the fairest that ever I did see,
I never did design to alter my mind,
Tho' you are below my degree.

In the merry month of June if my jewel will return,
Garlands of flowers then I'll have,
Lilies, pinks, and roses a garland I'll prepare,
And I'll wear it for my dear Johnson's sake.

Cf. 'The Irish Lovers' (no. 54). The races on the plain of Kildare were a
great gathering-place for people from all over Ireland.

67

Landlady Casey

Printed and sold by W. Collard, Bridewell-Lane, and Hotwells

The British Lion is my sign,
   A roaring trade I drive on,
Right English usage, neat French wine
   A landlady may thrive on;
At table d'hotte to eat and drink,
   Let French and English mingle,
And while to me they tip the chink,
   Faith, let the glasses jingle.

CHORUS

   Your rhino rattle,
   Come men and cattle,
Come all to Mrs. Casey:
   Of trouble and money,
   My jewel my honey,
I warrant I'll make you easy.

When drest and seated in my bar,
   Let 'squire, or beau, or belle come;
Let Captains kiss me if they dare,
   It's sir, you're kindly welcome!
On shuffle, cog, and slip, I wink,
   Let rooks and pidgeons mingle,
And if to me they bring the chink,
   Faith, let the glasses jingle.

Let love fly here on silken wings,
   His tricks I still connive at,
The lover who would say soft things,
   Shall have a room in private:
On pleasure I am pleas'd to wink,
   So lips in kisses mingle;
For while to me they bring the chink,
   Faith, let the glasses jingle.

cattle, whores (Partridge (1) notes this usage for late seventeenth–early eighteenth centuries). *shuffle, cog*, trick. *slip*, Partridge (1) records 'counterfeit coin', but only for *c.* 1596–1630. *rhino*, money. *rooks and pigeons*, tricksters and dupes. The tune 'Mrs. Casey', cited for nos 9 ('The Blue Lion') and 119 ('Unfortunate Billy'), is presumably the tune to which this ballad gave the name: the evidence suggests that this is a much earlier piece than either.

68

The last Farewel to the World, and Confession, of John Hogan, who is to be executed for the Wilful Murder of Ann Hunt

Ye servants all of each degree,
  And blooming virgins pretty,
Come listen to this mournful tale,
  A melancholy ditty;
Tis of a murder brought to light,
  A few months back was acted,
The wretch who did commit this deed,
  Justice hath now detected.

Ann Hunt, a blooming country girl,
  In Mary-le-bone lived a servant,
Near Portland-Place in Charlotte-street,
  At No. 4, subservient;
While the family to church were gone,
  To make their peace for heaven,
This maid was basely murdered,
  Condole her fate ye maidens.

John Hogan, a Mulatto man,
　　He was the wretch so sinful,
That did commit this bloody deed,
　　Quite piercing for to hear on;
After the maid he murdered,
　　And us'd as he thought proper,
He robb'd the house, and then made off,
　　Thinking his guilt to cover.

But mind how it was now found out,
　　For God will never smother,
No one that e'er commits [such] deeds,
　　The crying sin of murder;
In Newgate he was then confin'd,
　　And for transportation sentenc'd,
His harlot gay did him betray,
　　Lord grant him true repentance.

He then examin'd was straightway,
　　And by his own confession,
The marks of guilt so plain appear'd,
　　That when upon his trial,
He then could no denial make,
　　His frame o'erwhelmed with horrors,
The worst of deaths he deserves to die,
　　Example to all others.

And now he is try'd, cast, and condemned,
　　He could expect no other,
A just reward for villains base,
　　That delight to rob and murder:
On Newgate's scaffold he must die,
　　Unpitied and quite wretched,
And then to Surgeon's Hall convey'd,
　　And there to be dissected.

Written between 1788, when transportation began to Australia, and 1832, when dissection was abolished as part of the death-sentence; probably early in this period. *cast*, to find guilty. The striking block was not infrequently used for execution ballads.

69

Little Joe, The Chimney Sweeper

A New Song

They call me Little Joe, sir,
　A chimney sweep am I,
And tho' I'm reckon'd low, sir,
　I'm always mounting high;
My hands do clearly shew
　That dirty work's my trade,
But how much cash you know is
　Thus in London made.
How many deal in smoak,
　As I do ev'ry day,
Their sweepings never choak,
　They scrape and brush away;
Twixt me and gentle folk, sir,
　The diff'rence to be seen
Is, they without a joke, sir,
　Do dirty work more clean.
　　　　　　　　Sweep, sweep, soot O.

You cry, how black my face is,
　But Joe cares not a rush,
I'm fairer than some graces,
　'Cause never seen to blush;
My dirt in the right place is,
　More clean than others still,
A black face ne'er disgraces,
　A black heart always will.
For they who deal in smoak, etc.

My littleness conduces
　Your chambers clean to keep,
You seldom think what use is
　Poor Joe, the chimney sweep;

Tho' humble is my fare, sir,
  Yet I'm content, d'ye see,
My mind is free from care, sir,
  And that's enough for me.
For they who deal in smoak, etc.

Pray is it not uncivil
  For artists, as you know,
That when they draw a devil,
  They make him like poor Joe;
While others prone to evil,
  As imps, would better strike,
For as I never live ill,
  I can't be devil like.
Tis they who deal in smoke, etc.

probably late eighteenth-century or early nineteenth, when child sweeps
were in the public eye; and cf. a concert ballad 'Little Bess the Ballad
Singer', performed 1794. *deal in smoke*, swindle. *do dirty work more clean*, their
work means less physical dirt, but is dirty all the same (cf. Lamb's essay
'In Praise of Chimney-Sweeps'). Since the song is for a child singer, its
comparatively demanding nature indicates that it must surely be a concert
piece.

70

Lunardi

A New Song

Balloons they are all the rage,
   Nothing but them gives delight,
Lunardi's neck almost broke,
   The ladies were in a sad fright.

CHORUS

For there he went up, up, up,
   And there the balloon turn'd round-e
There all the gas flew out,
   And so he quickly came down-e.

Lunardi he is a fine man,
   To the ladies he gives much pleasure,
The tube of his air balloon
   Is surely a very great treasure.

CHORUS

There he went up, etc.

All the ladies they very much long
 To ride in his air balloon,
To taste love's sweetest joys,
 Be kiss'd by the man of the moon.

 CHORUS

 For there he went up, etc.

A lady was with him to ride,
 Frolick and frisk in the air,
But when his machine did fail,
 Was driven almost to despair.

 CHORUS

 For there he went up, etc.

Then he up by himself did go,
 Many feats he shew'd in the sky,
But his gas very fast running out,
 In the air he no longer cou'd fly.

 CHORUS

 For there he went up, etc.

Then near to the Adam and Eve,
 Lunardi's balloon came down,
We hope the next time he goes up,
 It may bring him much greater renown.

 CHORUS

 For there he went up, etc.

The balloon to the Pantheon went,
 Where the ladies all flock'd to enquire
The health of Lunardi their dear,
 Whose company they all desire.

 CHORUS

 For there he went up, etc.

Vicenzo Lunardi made the first aerial voyage by balloon in Britain (15 September 1784), from Moorfields in London to Standon in Hertfordshire. The refrain, presumably skitting Lunardi's Italian accent, is itself skitted in one or two later ballads. Cf. also no. 2 ('Air Balloon Fun'). Early balloons seem much to have invited the sexual analogy exploited here.

71

The Maid and Wife

[Sold at No. 42, Long-Lane]
Printed in 1794

Once I was a merry maid,
And merry did I become,
Meat and drink, and gay cloathing,
To be sure I wanted none.

CHORUS

A maid was I, and a maid was I,
Meat and drink, and gay cloathing,
To be sure, I wanted none.

I drest my head in the best fashion,
And on every finger a ring,
The worst handkerchief I had to my neck,
Cost me full five shilling.

My gown was made of the best of silk,
And pleated down to the ground,
The girdle that girded my waist about,
Cost me full twenty pound.

My stockings were made of the best of silk,
And garter'd up with a ribbon,
My shoes were made of the best of silk,
And both my buckles gilded.

One night as I lay on my bed,
And I lay fast asleep,
A young man stole my maidenhead,
Which caused me to weep.

CHORUS

And a wife was I, and a wife was I,
And a wife did I become,
Grief and care, sorrow and fear,
To be sure I wanted none.

I drest my head in the worst fashion,
And on never a finger a ring,
And the best handkerchief I had on my neck
Was not worth five farthings.

My gown it was made of the worst of wool,
And never a pleat thereon,
The girdle that girded my waist about
Was none but a leather thong.

My stockings were made of the worst of wool,
And garter'd up with a clout,
My shoes were made of the worst of leather,
And both the bottoms out.

Probably composed earlier than 1794. For further discussion see p. 9. This ballad has recently been recorded, with melody, in Birmingham (information supplied by Mr Thomson).

72

Maiden's Advice to get Married

Sold at No. 15, Long-lane, west Smithfield

Come all you brisk maidens, who husbands do lack,
I'd have you make haste, ne'er mind the new act,
New act nor new stile were ne'er good at first.
Take the man that you love 'for better or worse'.

They tell me my husband a tailor must be,
A tailor, good Lord! is no man for me,
His arse and his mouth so near it doth meet,
I think in my heart his breath can't be sweet.

His cabbage so strong my breath it would take,
His goose is so hard my teeth it wou'd break,
His knees knock together, his elbows so wide,
And so no poor tailor shall lay by your side.

My sister would have me to marry a craft
To hear the rogue's tricks would make you laugh,
When one shoe is done they the master will kick,
The thoughts of such days would make me quite sick.

The wife, with one shoe, kicks the landlord, good Sir,
Here's a groat for the landlord, and 2d for beer,
A halfpenny for 'bacco, a penny for bread,
Halfpenny for snuff to comfort the head.

The jolly blacksmith his hammer doth drive,
If he drives till he's blind he never will thrive;
His fire's so hot, and so thin is his coat,
That all that he gets won't cool his poor throat.

Some say that a butcher it is a good trade,
They're likely young men, and handsome blades,
If they blow up their wives as they blow up the veal,
I'd have the young lasses take care of their steel.

The jolly brisk weaver who works in the loom,
With his hands and his feet he plays you a tune,
The tune that he plays you is call'd pit-a pat,
He may weave himself blind before he gets fat.

The halfpenny barber your faces will trim,
While he takes hold of your nose and your chin,
The razor cuts hard, and the lathers bad made,
Such a barber's not fit to lather a maid.

So you pretty maids who husbands do want,
I'd have you take care, for MEN will grow scant,
For the wars they must have them, by land and by sea,
Johnny's the man who shall pleasure me.

An abridged but, so far as it goes, often superior version of the ballad next
following.

73

The Maiden's Choice

Come all you young women that husbands do lack
I'd have you make haste and ne'er mind the new act
New act or new stile was ne'er good at first,
Take the man that you love for better or worse.
　　To your own mind.

It was surely some cuckold contriv'd the new act,
Because that his daughter had made a contract,
And marry'd a man altho' he was poor,
It is the man that she lov'd and he did her adore.
　　To his own mind.

They say that a taylor my husband must be,
A taylor, good lord, he is no man for me,
His arse and his mouth so near they do meet,
I think in my heart his breath can't be sweet,
　　To my own mind.

His cabbage so strong my stomach won't take,
His goose is so hard my teeth it will break,
His knees knock together his elbows are wide,
And so no poor taylor shall lye by my side.
    To my own mind.

Likewise twice a day I chuse to drink tea,
My mother she did so before she had me,
With white bread and butter and sugar and cream,
To talk of a taylor it is a meer dream.
    To my own mind.

My sister she says I shall marry a craft,
To hear of their tricks it would make you to laugh,
When the shoe it is done their master they kick,
The thoughts of such doing will soon make me sick.
    To my own mind.

The wife with one shoe kicks the master good sir,
There's a groat for the landlord and two pence for her
A halfpenny for tobacco, a penny for bread,
And another for snuff to comfort her head.
    To her own mind.

The craft very close to his feet he sits down,
And then at rag fair buys his Doll a new gown,
And then for a fuddle between him and she,
Upon the high shelf the gown you may see.
    To your own mind.

The jolly blacksmith his hammer does thrive   [?drive
If he drives himself blind oh he never will thrive,
A fire so hot and so thin his coat,
And all he can get won't cool his poor throat,
    To his own mind.

You know that a butcher is a good trade,
They are merry lads O they are wanton blades,
If they blow up their wives as they blow up their veal
I'd have you young girls, take care of their steel.
    To your own mind.

They say that a jolly brisk sailor's the man,
At pleasing of girls they have a good hand,
When they come from sea they are jolly and free,
And all their wages they give unto me.
    To their own mind.

As for the sailors that venture their lives,
They bring home their gold to their sweethearts and wives.
They are jolly blades and forget dangers past,
And happily blest with their sweethearts and glass.
    To their own mind.

The jolly weaver that weaves in his loom,
With his hands and his heels he will play you a tune,
And the tune that he plays is called belly pat,
He may weave himself blind before he'll grow fat.
    To his own mind.

On Saturday night a weaver is rich
To handle a pot oh their fingers do itch,
There's Wednesday, Thursday, and Friday you see,
Forty poor weavers and ne'er a penny.
    To their own mind.

The bricklayer that on the scaffold does stand,
To bring him more mortar he calls to his man,
But bring him good ale for he works in the cold,
The roof is tiled and the house is sold.
    To his own mind.

Those halfpenny your face they do trim,   [?barbers
While they take you fast by the nose and the chin,
The razor goes hard the lather bad made,
Such a barber is not fit to lather a maid.
    To her own mind.

So you pretty maidens that husbands do want,
I'd have you make haste for men will grow scant,
The wars they must have them by land or by sea,
Johnny is the man that can pleasure me.
    To my own mind.

Composed *c.* 1753, the date of the Marriage Act which established the calling of banns and so prevented abductions. The *new stile* Gregorian calendar was adopted in 1751–2. A tailor's *cabbage* and *goose* is a shred of cloth, and a smoothing iron; but a ribald reference is also clear. A *fuddle* is a drinking bout (*OED*, 1813, however). Traditional humour at the expense of the tailor and his trade is here combined with another tradition, that of the song about the sexual prowess of the various kinds of artisan.

74

The Maiden's Moan,
For the Loss of her Sailor

One morning being fine, for to recreate my mind,
To walk was inclin'd by the side of a lee,
Tis Cupid with his art he selected out a dart,
Which pierced my tender heart, for my sweet sailor he.

He sung so melodious, his voice is harmonious,
His manly deportment is pleasant to me,
I am never at rest, for with care I'm opprest,
Love crowns my panting breast, for my sweet sailor he.

Confined to my chamber, my parents think no danger,
That I should love a stranger, and with him agree,
Tis because he's so poor that they turn him from the door,
Which grieves my heart full sore, for my sweet sailor he.

As I slept in slumber, had dreams out of number,
My heart was encumber'd, I think that I see
My lovely fine youth, or perfection and truth,   [?of
But wickedly I'm robb'd of my sweet sailor he.

Had I it in my power, with him I'd spend an hour,
All in some lonesome bower, where no one could I see,
Ye Gods above pray lend him, from stratagem defend him,
Unto my parents send him, he is my sweet sailor he.

The triads of feminine rhymes, and the occasional polysyllables, suggest
that this is a late eighteenth-century Irish ballad. See Introduction.

75

The Maid's Hopes in the Lottery

I am a young damsel that flatters myself,
That I shall grow rich in abundance of wealth,
I have got but one guinea, 'tis all I am worth,
And a fortunate girl I have been from my birth,
So I'll buy a ticket my hopes for to crown,
With flattery of the lottery of ten thousand pound.

My fortune was told me that I should be rich,
'Twas by an old woman, I think she's a witch,
For I've as good a chance as the best in the town,
To be a fine lady of fame and renown;
For in buying a ticket my hopes I will crown,
With flattery in the lottery of ten thousand pound.

Young Roger he swears that he loves me as dear
As if I was worth full three hundred a year,
But if I a lady of fortune should be,
Why should I accept such a fellow as he?
For in buying this ticket my hopes I will crown,
With flattery in the lottery of ten thousand pound.

Last night on my bed as I slumbring lay,
I fancied I heard them in Guildhall to say,
Here's number three thousand three hundred and one
I started and thought this great prize was my own
For in buying this ticket my hopes I will crown,
With flattery of the lottery of ten thousand pound.

Then many a nobleman should me approach,
And oftentimes take me abroad in his coach,
I'll wed the best bidder my fortune to raise,
Why should I look low when I have a great prize
For in buying this ticket my hopes I will crown
With flattery in the lottery of ten thousand pound.

But if that a blank should be drawn for me,
If my money I lose, still chearful I'd be,
For I can have Roger when at the last push,
One bird in the hand is worth two in the bush,
And if by my ticket no hopes should be found,
Farewel flattery of the lottery of ten thousand pound.

Perhaps written in the 1790s, when lotteries were held on a particularly large scale. They were virtually abolished in 1832. *flattery* is used in the sense of a (delusive) promise, an encouraging hope. *at the last push*, at a pinch. The block may show a contemporary stage-singer of the ballad who could perhaps be identified.

76

The Maids Resolution to follow her Love

There was a fair creature in the Islands did Dwell,
Was courted by a Captain & lov'd very well,
When her cruel Parents came it for to here,
They kept Madam Molly from her dearest dear.

One Night as Madam Molly lay musing in bed
A frolicksome fancy came into her Head,
Neither Father nor mother shall make me false prove
For I'll be a Soldier & follow my love.

She put a Coat & a pair of Breeches on
And deck'd herself in Aparel like a Man,
With a Case of Pistols and Sword by her side,
So like a Jolly Trooper Madam Molly did ride.

Madam Molly rode till she came to a Sea-port Town;
At the Sign of the Dreadnought she sat herself down,
The first that came in did unconstant prove,
But the next that appear'd was Mollys true love.

She said here's a Letter from Molly you adore,
And in this said letter is a Guinea or more,
For you & your Soldiers to drink her Health round,
Ay, that we will do Cry'd the Capt. G—d Zounds.

Madam Molly she held down her drowsey head
Saying fetch me a candle & shew me my Bed,
The Capt. reply'd, Sir, I lie at my Ease,
And you may lie with me sir if you please.

Sir, to lie with a Soldier is a difficult thing,
I am a new listed squire to fight for the King,
Next Morning Madam Molly arose,
And dress'd herself in her own feamale Cloaths

Saying here is your Molly whome you do adore,
She has ventur'd to follow you by Sea & shore,
Who has left her cruel Parents to sigh & Complain
Who would give Thousands & Thousands to see her again.

Now the Captain has marry'd her and calls her his Dear,
And settled upon her 500 a Year.
   Now, etc.

Date uncertain. *Sign of the Dreadnought*: dreadnought was first used (*OED*) in 1806, and here probably means a thick coat. The *guinea* ceased to circulate *c.* 1817. *new listed squire* probably means simply 'Esq.'. *Madam Molly*, from *c.* 1750 'Miss Molly' meant an effeminate man. The head block may be seventeenth-century.

77

The Merchant's Courtship to the Brazier's Daughter

An Old Song

As Jack was a walking in London city,
A viewing of the maidens so pretty,
By chance Jack heard some people say,
That Jack he in the streets must lay.

And Jack he heard of another pretty fancy,
A merchant courted a brazier's daughter Nancy,
And as he kept her company,
Agreed with her one night to stay.

You must tie a string unto your finger,
And let the end hang out of the window,
When I come and pull the string,
You'll come down stairs and let me in.

O now, says Jack, sure I may venture,
To pull the string out of the window.
So Jack he went and pull'd the string,
The brazier's daughter let him in.

Then up stairs Jack did retire,
He cock'd his pistol all for to fire,
The merchant came and found no string,
So he went home to bed again.

A-going home he flew into a passion,
A cursing all the women in the nation,
Says he, there is not one that's true,
And if there is tis very few.

It is in the morning when she awaked,
She tore her hair like one that was distracted,
To see Jack in his speck'd shirt,
With all his face daub'd o'er with dirt.

You dirty dog how came here?
You broke into my house, with such a treasure,
No, no, says Jack, I pull'd the string,
You came down stairs and let me in.

Now Jack and the brazier's daughter [wedded],
And every thing between them is contented,
Now they live in London-street,
Jack and the brazier's daughter I wot.

Printed with a 42 Long Lane block. *Jack* for a sailor suggests a date after
1700 (see Partridge (1)). For melody see *Journal of the English Folk-Song
Society*, vol. II (1905), p. 38, under the title 'Jack the Jolly Tar',

78

The Miraculous Hen or
Joan's Enquiry after a Cuckold's Cap

In Eden there liv'd a buxom young dame,
The wife of a miller, and Joan was her name,
And she had a hen of a delicate size,
The like was never beheld with eyes;
It had a red comb, green wings, yellow legs,
Each summer it laid her a bushel of eggs.

Then Joan was resolved to set her indeed,
Because she would have more of the same breed,
And as she was setting her hen one day,
A shepherd came by, and she to him did say,
I'm going to set my miraculous hen,
That I may have a bushel of eggs again.

Joan, said he, you must keep your eggs warm,
That they may prosper and come to no harm,
And to secure them from any mishap,
You must set your eggs in a cuckold's cap;
I've never a cuckold's cap, said she,
Yet nevertheless I'll be ruled by thee.

For this minute I'll trudge up and down,
And borrow one if there's one in town,
She went to the baker's wife, and to her did say,
Lend me your cuckold's cap, neighbour, I pray,
I'm going to set my miraculous hen,
And when I've done with it I'll bring it again.

The baker's wife turn'd to her, and thus reply'd,
If I'd such a thing it should not be deny'd,
You must go to my cousin that lives at the mill,
I know she had one, and may have it still;
Then strait to the house of the miller she went,
And told her that she by her cousin was sent,

To borrow a thing that was absolute rare,
A large cuckold's cap that her husband did wear,
I cannot deny but such a thing there may be,
But why should my cousin direct you to me?
These eighteen or nineteen years I've been wed,
My husband ne'er wore such a cap to his head.

You must go to the quaker that lives at the Swan,
And if she will lend it, I know she has one,
And if she will lend it you now for my sake,
I that favour for a kindness will take;
She went to the house of the great Yea and Nay,
And spoke to his wife who was buxom and gay.

Saying, I am come to borrow, if you please to lend
A large cuckold's cap, I was sent by a friend;
The quaker's wife turned and said with a frown,
I've not such a thing if you'd give me a crown,
For I would not lend it, supposing I had,
And that would make the cuckold run mad.

There's many a lass in town perhaps,
Who may be ingenious at making these caps,
But what they call them I cannot well say,
Therefore excuse me, good Joan, I pray;
When Joan being tir'd and fretted withal,
Said she, I've had no good fortune at all.

I think it is the beginning of sorrow,
To go up and down among neighbours to borrow,
A large cuckold's cap I'd have borrow'd indeed,
A small thing of value, but could not succeed,
But as I'm a woman, adzooks, cries Joan,
Before it is long I'll have one of my own.

set, to put a hen to sit on eggs; *sorrow . . . borrow*, adapting a proverb
(*ODEP*, p. 248). The amorousness of the Quaker, male or female, was a
stock eighteenth-century joke. A common name for a Quaker was a *yea-or-nay* man (see stanza 7).

79

Molly of the North Country

My love she was born in the North country wide,
Where's lofty hills and mountains all round on ev'ry side
She's one of the fairest creatures that ever my eyes did see,
She exceeds all the maids in the North country.

My parents separated me and my dear,
Which caus'd me to weep and shed many a tear,
Asleep I do mourn, and awake I do cry,
And tis all for the sake of my darling I die.

Come saddle my horse that I may go ride,
In search of my true love, let what will betide,
O'er lofty hills and mountains I'll wander and I'll rove,
In quest of my Molly, my own constant love.

My hand is scarce able my pen for to hold,
To write my love's praises in letters of gold,
She's teeth as white as ivory, and eyes as black as sloes,
And she's wounded my poor heart wherever she goes.

Had I all the riches of the African shore,
Or had I all the gold that the misers have in store,
Or had I all the riches that e'er my eyes did see,
I'd part with it all for my love's company.

My love she's as near as the bark to a tree,
My love she's as sweet as the cinnamon tree,
The top it will wither and the root will decay,
And a pretty maid's beauty it soon will fade away.

Perhaps early or at least incorporating snatches of early songs.

80

Mountains High

Printed by J. Davenport, 6, George's Court,
St. John's Gate, West Smithfield

One night upon my rambles from my belov'd again,
I met a farmer's daughter all on the lonesome plain
I said, my pretty fair maid, your beauty shines so clear,
All on this lonesome place, I'm glad to find you here.

I said, young man be civil, my company forsake,
And in my own opinion I think you are some rake,
But if my parents they should know, my life they will destroy,
For keeping of your company all on the mountains high.

It is true I am no rake brought up in Venus' train,
Or seeking for concealment all on the lonesome plain,
Your beauty so intic'd me I could not pass you by,
With my gun I will guard you all on the mountains high.

With that this pretty fair maid she stood all in amaze,
With eyes as bright as amber all on me she did gaze,
With cherry cheeks and ruby lips, she's the lass all for my eye,
She fainted in my arms, on the mountains high.

I did my best endeavour to bring her too again,
With that she kindly ask'd me I pray, sir, what is your name?
Go to yonder forest, my castle there you'll find,
Wrote in some lonesome history, call you for Randal Rine.

I said, my pretty fair maid, don't let your parents know,
For if you do they'll ruin me, and prove my overthrow;
And if that you should come for me, perhaps you will not find,
Go you to my castle, and call for Randal Rine.

Come all you pretty fair maids a warning take by me,
And do your best endeavour to shun bad company,
Or else, like me, you'll surely rue until the day you die,
Be warned of the lonesome roads all on the mountains high.

Irish, though printed in London. *Rine* = Ryan. For the melody see *Journal of the English Folk-Song Society*, vol. I (1899–1904), p. 271, under the title 'One Night upon my Rambles' (cf. the first line above).

81

The Mulberry Tree

Sung in the Stratford Jubilee

Behold this fair goblet, 'twas carv'd from the tree,
Which, O my sweet Shakespear, was planted by thee,
As a relick I kiss it, and bow at the shrine,
What comes from thy hand must be ever divine.
    All shall yield to the Mulberry Tree,
      Bend to thee,
      Matchless was he,
      Who planted thee,
    And thou like him immortal shall be.

Ye trees of the forest, so rampant and high,
Who spread round their branches, whose heads sweep the sky,
Ye curious exoticks, whom taste has brought here,
To root out the natives, at prices so dear.
    All shall yield, etc.

The oak is held royal, is Britain's great boast,
Preserv'd once our King, and will always our coast,
But of fir we make ships, we have thousands can fight,
While one, only one, like our Shakespear can write,
    All shall yield, etc.

Let Venus delight in her gay myrtle bowers,
Pomona in fruit trees, and Flora in flowers,
The garden of Shakespear all fancies can suit,
With the sweetest of flowers and fairest of fruit.
 All shall yield, etc.

With learning and knowledge the well letter'd Birch
Supplies law and physick, and grace for the church,
But law and the gospel in Shakespear we find,
And he gives the best physic for body and mind.
 All shall yield, etc.

The fame of the patron gives fame to the tree,
From him and its merits this takes its degree,
Let Phoebus and Bacchus their glories resign,
Our tree shall surpass both the laurel and vine.
 All shall yield, etc.

The genius of Shakespear outshines the bright day,
More rapture than wine to the heart can convey,
So the tree which he planted by making his own,
Has the laurels and bays, and the vine all in one.
 All shall yield, etc.

Then each take a relict of this hollow tree,
From folly and fashion a charm let it be,
Fill, fill to the planter the cup to the brim,
To honour his country do honour to him.
 All shall yield, etc.

The Stratford Jubilee was a celebration organized in honour of Shakespeare by David Garrick in 1769. Some time before the event, the clergyman then living in Shakespeare's own house in Stratford took a dislike to its mulberry-tree (believed to have been planted by the poet himself) and, much to the anger of the local people, had it felled. The tree was bought by an enterprising carpenter who carved the wood into various 'souvenir' shapes (the *fair goblet* of l.1); one of these was a box sent to Garrick enclosing the freedom of Stratford, which compliment inspired his organizing the Jubilee. A feature of the three-day event was the erection of an amphitheatre in the town on the plan of Ranelagh. For a further description of the Jubilee see Christian Deelman, *The Great Shakespeare Jubilee* (1964).

82

A new Dialogue between Mars and Venus

As Mars and Venus together were a walking,
It was in a cool and a shady air,
As Mars and Venus together were a talking,
It was in a cool and a shady bower,
Then I stepp'd forth and laid down by them,
They little thought that I was so nigh them,
As for to understand the matter,
Or the secrets of their talk,
Thus Mars did vapour as he walk'd.

Says Mars to Venus I am the God of battle,
And the chief General of the field,
I love to hear the great guns to rattle,
For I am arm'd with sword, spear and shield.
When I stepp'd forth, my strong invasion   [?by
I conquer all in city town and nation,
A champion bold none dare to resist me,
I conquer all wherever I go,
None dare refuse me nor yet say me no.

Alas says Venus, I think that you vapour,
There is a castle that ne'er yet was won,
The Mistress of it never drew a rapier,
Neither before it was ever a gun.
Tell me says Mars where this castle standeth,
In what town, or who the same commandeth,
I will reward you for your pains,
With some tokens of my love,
And doubtless I will in valour prove.

Thro' Venus's hall you may go through to it,
Underneath her cabinet that is the way to it,
Venus herself is the mistress of it,
It has no other defence than hair.
And I will hold you marks and pounds of it,
When once you come within the bounds of it,
You will come off with the loss of men,
Says more than that, you will be beat,   [?Nay
And it's ten to one but you do retreat.

Then Mars drew up his mighty army,
And fiercely charged against the fort,
Venus she began to parly, and him the reason for it,   [?ask him
Then remark, I needs must tell you,
The soldiers beat up a troop trevally,
Tit tat too, my boys, we have got it,
The great noble castle that never yet was won,
Nor never before it was ever a gun.

Alas! says Venus, my castle it is taken,
Before I was able to strike one blow,
Yet, nevertheless, if I am not mistaken,
I never felt such a pleasing FOE.
For my heart and my sense were all alivated   [elevated
And all my matters fairly estated,
This I will tell you as I am true,
Was the sweetest battle that ever I knew.

Irish. *vapour*, to talk grandiloquently. *trevally*, possibly a corruption of
'reveille' (often on drum and bugle).

83

A New Medly

Sung by Mr. Bannister at Drury-Lane, Theatre

If love's a sweet passion why should it torment, if bitter oh!
tell me tell me where I cast on Greenland caurse, in my arms [?shores
imbrace my Jenny of the green, my Jenny of the green groves the
rushes oh! green groves the rushers oh! the Parson kiss'd the
fiddlers wife, and could not preach for blushes oh, give my
wife a drink wholly oh fairly wholly oh fairly oh, give my
wife a drink and drive care away drink and drive care away we
ne'er go the sooner we ne'er go you warbling birds, go leave
me la le la de tis this shall be our halliday along the margin
of each stream, dear sylvia no longer cart me not court me not court
me not I am yet to young colin was the boniest swain that ever
pip'd on flowery plain and danc'd upon the curlherum bum, with
good english beer our songs we raise we have right by our born
charter, you promis'd our good fore fathers of old they were
roebust and stout and she lead me into her dubinalaro the
broom the bonny bonny broom his lose was my repose, I wish I
was with my dear swain, with his hound and the horn we'll
inliven the day and to the woods let us hasten away hast away

to the marry ton'd horn, calls the barbers all out in the morn,
then with hest to our shops we repair, to comb wigs and dress
the ladies hair, there all the day long this, this is our
song we never no never regard our hour, you promis'd two look
behold, there is four and twenty fidlers all of a row, it is
my ladies birth-day, therefore we'll keep holliday and we are
come here to be merry, merrily shall we live now under the
blosom that hangs on the bough how pleasing is beauty how
sweet is her charms how delightful her imbraces how pleasing her
charms, sure there's nothing so easy as learning to love it is
tough us on earth and by all things above, and to beauty's bright
standard, all heros must yeild, tis beauty that conquors and
steep the fair feild.   [?sweeps

The whole text is composed of snatches from songs familiar at the time.
We have not attempted to 'correct' the spelling, since some of its irregulari-
ties must be intentional (e.g. *marry-toned horn*). *curlherum bum*, possibly what
Partridge (1) calls the 'female pudend'; but the phrase is obscure. The
block is of great interest as apparently showing a street ballad-singer
selling 'garlands'.

84

A New Song

Come all you roaring boys,
  Why will you stay at home,
Go kill the Greenland Whales,
  Which cause the seas to foam.
For the seas they are deep
  And a mighty long way,
And it is of a Greenland Whale,
  That has caused me to rue.

How can i leave my true love,
  How can i leave my dear,
For to cross the raging seas,
  To a place i know not where.
And don't you be faint hearted,
  I am oblig'd to go,
To cross the raging seas
  To a place i do not know.

And when we came to the eastern banks
  Our fingers for to blow,
And when we came to the western banks
  Our land we did not know.
But be you all stout hearted,
  Let not your courage fail,
And i'll warrant you my boys,
  We'll bring home a Greenland Whale.

191

And when we came to the Greenland banks
　　The spouts they did rise,
Stand you bug and make ready,
　　Our captain he did cry
Stand you bug and make ready,
　　Let not your courage fail,
And i'll warrant you my boys,
　　We will bleed this Greenland Whale.

My service to Philidelphia,
　　For that is a pretty place,
And likewise to my true love
　　I long to see her face.
With the wind at east north east,
　　A sweet and pleasant gale,
And i'll warrant you my boys,
　　We'll bring home a Greenland Whale.

The references to Philadelphia, and to the 'north-east trades' in the last stanza, imply that this is an American ballad.

85

A New Song

Newgate market's the subject I have for to say,
Dedicated to wives that are buxom and gay,
Now you that are like her I'll soon make you run,
But the virtuous the good dames, I know will buy one.
    O the butcher, etc.

Her husband he said I am going to sup,
And there I suppose love, we shall keep it up,
And if I should stay there until it is late,
I will not disturb you but go to the gate.

She hearing her husband these words for to say,
Directly she sent for her lodger straitway,
Saying pray thee come home for to bed we're intent,
I'll presently come was the answer he sent.

Directly the butcher went home as 'tis said,
And pull'd off his cloaths for to go into bed,
When just at that instant she call'd in a fright,
My lamp it is out butcher bring up your light.

Then he paddl'd up stairs and he lighted her lamp,
Just then his poor leg it was siez'd with the cramp,
So he sat while she rub'd it, and then with a smile,
She said my dear butcher my lamp it wants oil.

So he oil'd it and trim'd it unto her desire,
She cry'd my dear boy push the cotton up higher,
To draw up the oil for to give us more light,
So he gave it a push, she said now it is right.

But here is the joke now how great the surprize,
The lamp burn'd so brisk that it dazzled her eyes,
And made them both sleepy the thing is well known,
For contented they lay till her husband came home.

But her husband sweet Billingsgate he did not see,
But got into the house by the help of his key,
And pull'd off his cloaths for to get into bed,
And the first thing he felt was the strong butcher's head.

He began to baste him for what he had done,
He wak'd in a fright and down stairs he did run,
The fish man pursu'd him quite into the street,
For mad men or spirits they took them that see it.

The fishman return'd and he siez'd on his gold,
While the butcher his pitiful case did unfold,
A good natur'd watchman he lent him a coat,
Others, shoes and stockings and breeches to boot.

But the cash of the butcher was in his own room,
Which made the poor fishman return it quite soon,
But threatens to sue him, now beef at him scorns,
And says I've got my money, and you've got the horns.

Stanza 2 would appear to be missing from this version. Line 6, Partridge (1) records *keep it up* in this sense 'from ca. 1780'. *the gate*, Billingsgate. *that see it*, 'that saw it'. The block shows a cuckold with horns being led (on a chain) 'by the nose'. The tail-block would appear to show a harrow and a curry-comb.

86

A New Song

Steward

Mr Goodman goodmorrow pray how do you do
I have just heard some news but i hope it's not true
Jemmy wheedle he told me and firmly declares
You have hired jack hartwell for just seven years.

Farmer

Mr Steward the news that you heard it quite true   [?it's
And i think i have done the best thing i could do
He can reap he can mow he can plow he can cart
No labour he values but has got a sound heart

But i would beg a favour Daddy Goodman to day,
And desire you would turn that jack hartwell away
From my good master's mother you get a reward
It will please her i know and likewise my lord

I value no pleasings, i owe him no rent
And hartwell shall stay sir, i am fully bent
I have hired the man Sir, and that is thing   [?the thing
And to turn him away sir, i would not for the king

Don't tell me of kings for my will shall be done
You shall turn him away sir let it be right or wrong
Let's have none of your frowns, sir, but pray be content
Or you'll turn out yourself sir, or i double your rent

Mr. Steward this usage i can't understand,
I'll get up and go to my lord out of hand
You shall double my rent, sir, or i shall turn out
I'll hop to my lord to know what its about,

Po, po, Daddy Goodman dont be in a passion
The words i just hinted at court is the fashion
Turn hartwell away it will answer the plan
And my lord his own self shall send you a man,

Mr. Steward i find now my servants you'll chuse
Or by double oppression my farm i must lose
I can show you a book and it plainly appears
We have chose our own servants for some hundred years

Daddy Goodman the Times they are altered its plain
And to talk of your books it must be in vain.
It is my lord's pleasure that things shall be so
And his will shall be done all the tenant shall know

Bad lords and bad stewards i am sorry to hear it
My cheese it is hard and i must grin and bear it
To crush Magna Charta it is their endeavour
May such lords and such stewards be Damn'd all Together

Probably later eighteenth-century, and printed almost without punctuation as here.

87

A New Song

Tune—What a Pox wou'd you be at

Ye all may depend,
I am liberty's friend,
And I'll lay any Scotchman a tester,
That Wilkes will do things,
Worth the notice of kings,
And make us all rich by next Easter.

He'll make a great rout,
And he'll find some knaves out,
With vigour he'll strongly oppose 'em.
For the good of the nation,
He'll make an oration,
And in the newspapers disclose 'em.

In Punch's grand shew,
Ye have seen in a row,
Fine figures composed of wax-work,
It's rogues such as these,
Have schem'd by degrees,
The mischief of all our tax work.

The matter's quite clear,
As witness strong beer,
For that shou'd be never concealed,
But Wilkes is the man,
Who will if he can,
Soon get the strong beer act repealed.

From the head to the foot,
He has maul'd my Lord ——   [Bute
Nobody of this need acquaint him,
But we're told that the devil's,
More handsome and civil,
Than people are pleas'd for to paint him.

I heartily wish,
That again in his dish,
Folks may'nt throw such cart loads of scandal,
Because he may mend,
And be liberty's friend,
Then Wilkes will no longer him handle.

He's a dull empty ass,
That won't fill up a glass,
For Wilkes, both without doors & in doors,
But I vow and declare,
'Twas a foolish affair,
To break all the Mansion house windows.

The much-resented tax on beer was introduced in 1767. The reference in the last line is to the occasion of Wilkes' being returned as Member of Parliament for Middlesex. When the result of the voting was obvious, the mob returning to London demanded that all house lights be lit in celebration; the Lord Mayor refused to comply and an attack on the Mansion House windows resulted. The tail-block, through lack of space, was printed sideways in the original.

88

A New Song, Called Harry Newell

When I came to this town,
 They call'd me Harry Newell,
Now they've chang'd my name,
 And they call me the raking Jewel.
  Fal lal, etc.

They put me to bed,
 Thinking I was weary:
Sleep I could get none,
 For thinking of my deary.

All the night awake,
 All the day am weary:
Sleep I can get none,
 When I think of my deary.

Her cheeks are ruby-red,
    Her lips are like a cherry;
Her eyes as black as a sloe,
    And her hair as brown as a berry.

She is a lovely lass,
    She has my heart in keeping:
When I go to bed,
    She hinders me from sleeping.

I'll send my love a letter,
    And I will entreat her:
In Belfast-town with speed,
    I will be sure to meet her.

Down by the Ropery,
    All thro' mud and mire;
Down by Hampster-Place,
    There liv'd my heart's desire.

She was a beauty bright,
    There's no one can excell her;
She was my heart's delight,
    I know not what befel her.

Northern Irish. *OED* first records *rake* in this sense (see stanza 1) for 1700.
ropery, a rope-walk. A very fine ballad.

89

Paddy's Departure

Don't blubber dear Norah I beg yo'll be easy,
For soon you will see your fond Paddy again,
Returning with laurels, with liberty crazy,
An eye or two less or a limb or two lame.

CHORUS

Sing ditheru, how d'ye do Patrick Shelaly?
To the right about, fight it out all the day long,
Cut and flash, Frenchmen hash, pop away gaily,
Suck away, while you may, whisky so strong.

I'm going to beat all the Frenchmen my jewel,
Because they presume to make laws of their own,
They want all men to be equal, that would be d—— cruel,
For then each great monarch must jump from his throne.

Then what d'you think of their roguish Convention?
They plunder'd the bishops because they were poor,
Depriv'd every knave of his title and pension,
And turn'd all the nuns and monks out o'door.

Their priests have come over to live by subscription
No doubt 'tis much better than feeding on frogs
I'd make them a gift of a better description,
By subscribing a halter a piece to the dogs.

Of treason they think a king can be guilty,
Their own they condemned for not keeping his word,
They say to their subjects all kings should swear fealty;
Not their subjects of them, Oh! monstrous absurd.

And what exceeds all their former transgressions
They've trampl'd on king-craft, and pull'd down her throne,
Let's unite with the Austrians, Prussians, and Hessians,
As we're without sin, let us cast the first stone.

Now let's drink success to those great northern heroes
Empress Kate, Prince Coburg, and brave Duke of York,
So Citizens Francois! mind how you come near us,
Or expect to be all cut in pieces like pork.

An anti-'Loyalist' Irish ballad of the later 1790s.

90

Patrick Flemming

Patrick Flemming was a Vallient Soldier,
He carried his Blunderbuss upon his shoulder
He cockt his Pistol and drew his Rapier,
Stand and deliver for I am the taker fal, lal,

If you're Patrick Flemming as I suppose you be,
We are three Pedlars a ganging so free sir,
We are three Pedlars a ganging to Dublin,
Nothing at all in our Pockets but our loading.

Says Patrick Fleming prithe don't trifle,
For I am resolved Your packs for to rifle,
Here is a bank on which they may rest on,
To search them all I have a Commission.

Loath they were to do as he commanded,
But knowing Patrick charg'd double-handed,
Searching their packs most carefully round,
There did he find four Hundred pound.

Oh! I have two brothers they're both in the army
The one is at Cork and the other at Kilkenny,
If they were here both blyth and bonny,
I'd rather see them than any one dear honey.

As I was going over Ruberry mountain,
Gold and silver there was counting
He thought it little I thought it better,
I took the Gold from Colonel Pepper.

My Whore she proved false and that is the reason
Or else Patrick Flemming had never been taken,
When I was asleep and knew nothing of the matter
Then she loaded my arms with Water:

Oh Patrick Flemming how often have I told you
With Swords with Pistols we would surround You,
For kissing of other mens wives brisk and merry,
as You was going to Londonderry.

Now my dear brothers i must leave You,
For of my Life they will bereave me
But when he set his foot upon the Ladder
He briskly called for his hat and Feather.

Now You pretty Wives of fair London City
E'er it is long I sure shall be with Ye,
So bold and so Gallant i'lle gane to ye
That halters not made that [are] can undo me.   [?e'er

91

Paul Jones

T. Birt, Printer, No. 39 Great St. Andrew Street, Seven Dials

An American Frigate from New York she came,
She mounted guns forty, called the Rachael by name,
For cruising the channel of old England's fame,
Our noble commander, Paul Jones was his name.

We had not sail'd far before we espied,
A large forty-four and a twenty likewise,
With a large fleet of merchantmen loaded with store,
And the convoy stood in for the old Yorkshire shore.

At twelve o'clock at midnight, we hove alongside,
With a large speaking trumpet, from whence came he cry'd
Come answer me quickly, I have hail'd you before,
Or else a broadside into you I will pour.

We engaged them five glasses, five glasses so hot,
'Till fifty bright seamen lay dead on the spot,
And forty more of them lay bleeding in their gore,
While the shot from the Rachael so smartly did pour.

Our gunner being frightened, to Paul Jones did say,
Our vessel leaks water since fighting to day,
When up spoke Paul Jones in the height of his pride,
When we can't fight no longer we will sink alongside.

It's now my brave boys we have taken a prize,
A long forty-four and a twenty likewise;
God help their parents they have caused for to weep,
For the loss of their sons in the ocean so deep.

Paul Jones (1747–92) was an American naval officer. In September 1778 he commanded two French ships, the *Pallas* and the *Bonhomme Richard* (the *Rachael* of this ballad) in an engagement with two British men-of-war off Flamborough Head. The *Bonhomme Richard* sank after the desperate battle described here in which Jones compelled the English ships to surrender.

92

Mr. Peter Shaw, The Handsome Footman's Sorrowful Lamentation, and last Farewel to his Wife and Child

I pray draw near, attend to me,
Who soon must suffer on the tree,
A wretched tale I'll now unfold,
Caus'd by the lucre of cursd gold;
In wicked paths I then did stray,
Which caus'd my fall,
Take warning all; well-a-day.

From Mr. Stanhope plate I stole,
The Lord have mercy on my soul,
Christ look down and pardon me,
When I do front the fatal tree.
In wicked paths I once did stray, etc.

Weep not for me my dearest Wife,
The law doth take my forfeit life,
A widow, orphan it doth make,
That thought's enough my heart to break,
In wicked ways I once did stray, etc.

O God ador'd, my soul pray save,
A father prove to my dear babe,
When in the dust I then do lie,
May he in vain for bread ne'er cry.
In wicked paths I once did stray, etc.

My tender babe thou smil'st on me,
Not knowing of my misery,
My child I hope will never know,
The grief which I now undergo.
In wicked paths I once did stray, etc.

Dear Wife my infant child pray rear,
The Lord above to love and fear,
When I to folly first did run,
Alas! I quickly was undone.
In wicked paths I once did stray, etc.

When in my coffin I am laid,
There's one to death by sin betray'd,
Pray tell my child, if he should weep,
His father only is asleep.
In wicked paths I once did stray, etc.

A parting kiss I'll take my dear,
Why on thy cheek doth fall that tear?
There's many on the gallows die,
Whose souls to Heaven I trust did fly.
In wicked paths I once did stray, etc.

O God thou powerful being high,
Cleanse my soul before I die,
Jesus Christ I pray look down,
Prepare for me a heavenly crown.
In wicked paths I once did stray, etc.

93

The Pleasures Of a Country Life

How melancholy crows the cock,
I heard the sound of the village clock,
The dairy maid she's beneath the cow,
While Roger's whistling at the plough;
If these be pleasures you delight,
Farewel me from a country life.

The poor man thrashes all day in the barn,
Thrashing and toiling, and thinking no harm,
At night he comes home, quite tir'd from his labour,
He takes his short pipe, and he smoaks with his neighbour;
If these be the pleasures you delight,
Fare you well me, from a country life.

The team comes home, the ploughboy he whistles,
The great dog he barks, the turkey cock grisles,
The ravens they croak, the magpies they chatter,
Quack! quack! say the ducks as they swim on the water;
If these be pleasures you delight,
Fare you well me from a country life.

The hogs they grunt for grains and swill,
Up comes the dairy maids, calling for Will,
To feed the fat ducks, and to keep them from brawling.
The geese and the turkies are always a squalling;
If these be pleasures you delight
Fare you well me from a country life.

We feed on butter milk, curds, and whey,
God deliver me from it! I heartily pray,
The ravens they croak, the magpies they chatter,
Quack! quack! say the ducks, as they swim on the water;
If these be the pleasures you delight,
Fare you well from me a country life.

Possibly early, and in the tradition of 'Come Live with Me and be my Love' and all its successors. *grisle*, probably grizzle, to grumble, fret.

94

The Plowman's Glory

As I was walking one morning in the spring,
I heard a young Plowman most sweetly to sing,
And as he was singing, these words he did say,
No life like a Plowman in the month of May.

The lark in the morning she rises from her nest,
And mounts in the air with the dew round her breast,
And with the jolly Plowman she'll whistle and sing,
And at night she'll drop into her nest again.

If you walk in the fields any pleasure to find,
You may see what the Plowman enjoys in his mind,
There the corn he sees grow, and the flowers spring,
And the Plowman's as happy as a prince or king.

When his days work is done that he has for to do,
Perhaps to some country wake he will go,
There with his sweet lass he will drink and sing,
And at midnight return with his lass back again.

And as they return from the wake to the town,
Where the meadow is mow'd and the grass is cut down
If they chance to stumble upon the green hay,
Tis kiss me now or never the damsel will say.

Then he rises next morning to follow his team,
Like a jolly young plowman so neat and so trim,
If he kisses a pretty girl he will make her his wife,
And she loves a young plowman as dear as her life.

Come Molly and Sue, lets away to the wake,
There's the Plow-boys will treat us with ale and cake;
And if coming they should gain their ends,   [?home
Ne'er fear but they'll marry us to make us amends.

There's Molly and Dolly, and Nelly and Sue,
There's Ralph, John and Will, and young Tommy too,
Each Lad takes his Lass to the Wake or the Fair,
Adzooks they look rarely I vow and declare.

The sub-title, 'A new Song', suggests that this may be a concert-piece:
which is somewhat confirmed by the roseate sentiments, but perhaps not
by the diction. *wake*, annual parish festival, holiday. *adzooks*, god's hooks
'mid-c.18–mid-c.19' (*Partridge* (1)). For a melody (and much 'edited'
text) see R. Vaughan Williams, *Folk Songs from the Eastern Counties*, n.d.,
p. 19: 'The Lark in the Morning'.

95

The Poesy of Thyme

A New Song

In Stafordshire I was born,
   Near Newcastle-Under-Line,   [Lyme
But the pretty maidens all laugh me to scorn,
   For my wearing the Poesy of Thyme.

It was in the time of the year
   When the Thyme it grew wild;
It was just in the heighth of my bloom,
   When my false love he got me with child.

But now he is gone to the sea,
   He has blasted me just in my prime;
I never more shall him see,
   So I'll wear the sweet Poesy of Thyme.

For the time will go swiftly along,
    And time for no man will stay,
May the time and the tide be his guide,
    And send my true love unto me.

If fortune proves to me severe,
    And I should never see him more,
I'll wear the sweet Poesy of Thyme,
    For the false man whom I adore.

Young maidens take warning by me,
    Lest ye are cropt in the height of your prime;
And are forced to sing lullaby,
    And like me wear the Poesy of Thyme.

poesy = posy. For the treatment of this theme in ballad literature more
generally, see Reeves, *The Idiom of the People* and *The Everlasting Circle*.

96

The Poor Whores Complaint

Come listen a while and you shall hear,
   How the poor Whores fares in the winter
They've hardly got any rags to hide their ware
   Indeed tis a despret thing Sir.
With their draggel tales thats nine inches deep,
   And hardly a shooe or a stocking,
Yet if a Cull they by chance should meet,
   At him they will be bobing.
Say Molly I think my case very hard,
   For I can get no Money;
Says Nancy I think that mines as bad,
   For last night I yarnt but a penny.
All night we stand freezing in the Cold,
   With our cul til the constable he comes early
Then he packs us away[. . .]
   So we pay for Whoreing sevearly.
Says Sally I think I've the worst luck of you all;
   Since I have known Whoreing,
I ne'er in my life before went without a Smock,
   Altho it was nare such a poor one.
Altho' I'm trudging the streets al night in the cold
   My rags Men are puling and haling.
Old Nick I'm sure would not be a Whore,
   is grown such a Devil of a caling   [?It's
Straightway young Nelly reply'd,
   What signifies complaining,
You know you're all poxt and so am I,
   And that indeeds our failings.
We swarm like Bees at every street end,
   Ca[t]ching at every fellow,
Let him be ever so poxt or Clean,
   We're always ready him to folow.
This . . . that tradings so dead,   [?is because
   We are seen to be so Common.
Tis enough to make us all mad,

Sure we are not Like other Wemen.
Theres some Wemen are so Plagey sly,
   Tho you shal strive to provoke them,
They look as if butter would not melt in their Mouths,
   But dam them chese wont choak them.
Theres some that goes in Silks and Satins gay,
   Tis them that gets the Money;
With their next nabour they will slyly play,
   And cal him their Joy and their Honey.
While he with Money can supply,
   They are always ready to serve him,
While his poor wife and Children at home,
   Does Live and for bread are almost starving.
Likewise all you men that have hansome wives
   Take care they dont forsake you,
For if they want money as sure as you've Lives,
   They will a Cuckold make you.
They'll graft such a pair of horns on your head
   That you can hardly bare them,
They are such cunning Jades if hou hant a are   [?care, *or* eare
   They will force you for to ware them.
Before those privet whore was known,   [?privy whores
   In town to be so plenty,
We common girls had better Luck;
   Then men were not so dainty.
They brought to us brave English quine
   Of which we would bite and pinch them,
If we set them on fire at both ends,
   The devil he may quench them.

Draggel tale (also) name for a whore. *cul*, man, partner. *quine* (last line but three) is probably 'quills': cf. no. 107 'Sally Mac Gee', l.23, where the context is the same and the meaning obvious. *set on fire*, poxed. Possibly seventeenth-century, and a hauntingly realistic account of the whore's life.

97

The Postboy

A New Song

I'm a Hounslow young lad, and Tidy's my name,
Full many a job have I drove,
Yet never cross'd nag that was windgall'd or lame,
But always had such as would move;
A tight pair of buckskins, and boots jetty black,
My spurs ever polish'd and smart,
A trim little jacket to put on my back,
Was always the pride of my heart.

A good ten miles an hour in common my pace,
Where leaving behind ev'ry rip,
They try to put by, but I lead them a chace,
And tip 'em the smack of the whip;
When oft as I'm driving along in this stile,
Thro' many a town as I go,
The girls of each inn will bestow me a smile,
Their meaning I very well know.

Then I find 'em a rig whenever I call,
And loll at my ease on return,
I laugh and I jeer, and I talk with 'em all,
But Patty's my only concern;
At an inn near to Windsor this little rogue dwells,
Well known by her nice winning air,
That all other girls of the place she excels,
And is cal'd pretty Patty the Fair.

We have both made a vow, should we get the stuff,
To marry and so become one,
As others have done, for tis common enough,
We'll set up an inn of our own;
Then she'll be call'd Madam, and I'll be call'd Sir,
We'll stick up the sign of the Star,
Mongst postboys and waiters I'll bustle and stir,
While Pat hollows loud in the bar.

Presumably a concert-song, reminiscent of Dibdin. Some of the details suggest a late eighteenth-century date. *crossed*, ridden. *rip*, an inferior, worthless horse (*OED*, 1778). *rig*, 'a mischievous or wanton act'. Partridge (1) suggests that *stuff* was not used to mean 'money' until the 1770s, which fits the general fast-mail-coach idea of the piece.

98

The Prevailing Fashion, Or,
the World turned upside down

Good people all I pray draw near,
In country and in town, sir,
Their pride is got to such a pitch,
The world's turn'd upside down, sir;
They are contriving every day,
Their pretty shapes to spoil, sir,
Short waisted gowns they now do wear,
Their hump backs for to hide, sir.

CHORUS.

So you ladies of the fashion too,
Adhere unto my censure,
I have short bodied gowns now for sale,
And very pretty spencers.

The servant girls they imitate,
Their pride in every place, sir,
And if they have a flower'd gown,
They'll have it made short waisted;
They'll have it rump'd up all behind,
It hangs just like a wallet,
With a scull cap upon their heads,
Just like a Scotchman's bonnet.

Twas in London you shall hear,
Upon a certain day, sir,
A lady she was dressed up,
A going to the play, sir;
The blust'ry winds did blow so hard,
Blew off her caps and wig, sir,
With her muff and tippet round her neck,
She look'd like a hairy pig, sir.

These low heel'd slippers they do wear,
Their gouty legs to shew, sir,
Their petticoats are fring'd round,
They cut a tearing shew, sir;
And when their bosoms you do view,
The truth I do declare, O.
A modesty they all will have,
If never a smock to wear O.

The farmers daughters in every place,
The truth I do lay down, sir,
They dress more grand I do declare,
Than ladies of renown, sir;
A hat and feather they must have,
And a mask all o'er they faces,   [their
It is hop'd their pride it will come,
To linsey woolsey dresses.

spencers date from 1803 (*OED*). In general, the account of the prevailing fashions and the reference to the farmers' vulgar prosperity suggest an early nineteenth-century date. A *modesty* is a veil to cover the bosom. Satire against bare bosoms and veiled faces occurs often elsewhere.

99

The Rakes of Stony Batter

Come all you roving blades, that ramble thro the City,
Kissing pretty Maids, listen to my Ditty,
Our time is coming on, when we will be merry,
Kitty, Poll, and Nan, will give us Sack and Sherry.
     Hey for Bobbin Joan, Hey for Stony Batter,
     Keep your Wife at home or else I will be at her.

There's Bridget, Peg, and Nell, with Nancy, Doll, & Susan,
To please their sweethearts well, sometimes will go a boozing,
But when their cash is gone, they'll hunt for a Cully,
And bring their splinters home, to their beloved Bully.
     Hey for Bobbin Joan, Hey for Stony Batter, etc.

In Summer Lasses go, to the Fields a Maying,
Thro' the Meadows gay, with their Sweethearts playing,
Their smiling winning ways, shewe for game their willing,
Tho' Jenny cries nay, I won't F——k for a shilling.
     Hey for Bobbin Joan, Hey for Stony Batter, etc.

Go you cunning Knave, no more of coax nor wheedle,
By those Buttons in my Sleve, I'll prick you with my needle,
What will you still be bold, Mammy call to this Man,
For shame my hands don't hold, I vow my breath is just gone.
　　　Hey for Bobbin Joan, Hey for Stony Batter, etc.

There's Joan a buxom Lass, met with lusty Johnny,
They went to take a glass, he call'd her dear and honey,
She said you silly Clown, take me round the middle,
Play me Bobbin Joan, or else I'll break your fiddle.
　　　Hey for Bobbin Joan, Hey for Stony Batter, etc.

He gently laid her down, and he pull'd out his scraper,
He play'd her such a tune, which made her fart and caper;
She said my dearest John, your such a Jolly rover,
My cloak and gown I'll pawn, that you would ne'er give over.
　　　Hey for Bobbin Joan, Hey for Stony Batter, etc.

Come let us take a roam, up to Stony Batter,
Keep your Wife at home, for humpers will be at her,
Hey for cakes and ale, Hey for pretty misses,
That will never fail, for to crown our wishes.
　　　Hey for Bobbin Joan, Hey for Stony Batter,
　　　Keep your Wife at home or else I'll stop her water,
　　　　Is your apples ripe, are they fit for plucking,
　　　Is your maid within, ready for the F——g.

Stony Batter is a quarter of Dublin. *cully*, a dupe (here). *splinters*, scraps. *fiddle*, usually the female, but here the male 'pudend' (see *Partridge* (1), who gives 'from ca.1800' for the usual meaning: but as a metaphor the expression is both likely and dateless; cf. *scraper* in the next verse). *hump*, to have intercourse (Partridge (1), ca. 1760–1800). *cakes and ale*, a familiar phrase from Shakespeare's *Twelfth Night*. *Bobbin Joan* seems to represent the tutelary spirit of coition ('bobbin' often carries a ribald sense). The bowdlerized printing in our text follows that in the original.

100

Remember Jack

Composed by Mr. Dibdin, sung by Mr. Fawcett

When scarce a hand-spike high,
Death with old dad made free,
So what does I do me, but I
Pikes it off to sea;
Says I to sweetheart Poll,
If ever I come back,
We'll laugh and sing, tol de rol lol,
If not, remember Jack.

I'd fortune smooth and rough,
The wind would chop and veer,
Till hard knocks I'd nap'd enough,
On board a privateer;
Propt with a wooden peg,
Poll I though would bid me pack,
So was forc'd, d'ye see, to beg,
And 'twas pray remember Jack.

I ax't as folks hove by,
And shew'd my wooden pin,
Young girls would sometimes sigh,
And gaping lubbers grin;
In vain I'd often bawl,
My hopes were ta'en aback,
And my share of coppers small,
So pray remember Jack.

One day, my lockers bare,
And togs all tatter'd grown,
I twigg'd a pinnace fair,
Well rigg'd, a bearing down;
Twas Poll, she look'd so spruce,
What thus, say she, come back,
My tongue forgot its use,
And pray remember Jack.

What matters much to prate,
She'd shiners sav'd a few,
Soon I became her mate,
Wan't Poll a sweetheart true?
Then a friend I'd sarv'd before,
From a long voyage trips back,
Shar'd with I his gold galore,
For he well remember'd Jack.

So what tho' I lost my leg,
It seem'd to fortune mend,
And was forc'd, d'ye see to beg,
I gain'd a wife and friend;
Here's the King, Old England, Poll,
My shipmate just come back,
Then laugh and sing, tol de rol lol,
And pray remember Jack.

pike, depart. *nap*, to receive severe punishment (*OED*). *shiners*, coins (*Partridge* (1)). Vivid, gay, deft—and smug: very Dibdinesque.

Resolute Dick

I'll tell you of a comical Jest,
Of a Countryman that came out of the West,
Who came up to London to see my Lord Mayor,
And abundance of fine Folks that seem'd to lie there.
    Then up to the City the Ploughman did range,
To see the fine Folks in their rich golden change;
And he above all did admire more strange,
To see the fine Folks at the Royal Exchange.
    This Countryman amazed did stand,
And walked about with his whip in his Hand;
In come a fine Fellow a don of the Town,
And call'd him a Bumkin and Country Clown.
    Then ask'd him how he dare to presume,
To loiter and laughter, and fill up the room;
Amongst the gay Ladies with Silks and perfume,
Be gone & pack off, or else the stocks is your doom.
    Fine Fellow says he, I care not a Fig,
For all your high Words, and your looking so big;
I'm come for to see my Lord Mayor's good Grace,
And I care not for the angry frowns of your Face.
For as long as I list I'll stay in this place,
Or on your gay coat I'll lay my long Lash.
    This fine fellow began to be in a Passion indeed,
And thus the whole Quarrel began to proceed;
With making an Offer to give him a Kick,
The ploughman received it just in the Nick;
And he told his Name was resolute Dick,
He up with his Whip and gave him a lick.
    Then this fine Fellow began to roar,
And ask'd the Clown how he dare to do it;
Then presently came in twenty or more,
As he was a Person of Repute.
    He abus'd me first and call'd me a Clown,
I could not forbear but give him a Frown,
Why should Londoners run Countrymen down,

You can't live without us in city or town.
    Ploughman I would have you to understand,
We have both Silver and Gold at Command;
Rubies and Jewels, nay Diamonds and Rings,
All Sorts of Spices and other fine things.
Of many rich Coffers we carry the Keys,
Therefore to tell we live at our ease;
We eat and we drink and we walk were we plese,
What do you think of such Fellows as these.
    For all your Jewels you may starve or die,
Did we not bring you a daily Supply,
We harrow we mow we plow we sow,
And we have both Milk and Honey you know;
Therefore to blame us you're something too bold,
You'd starve if you fed on Silver and Gold,
We have corn, Cattle and Sheep in the Fold,
Rich bacon and Beans as our bellies will hold,
    We daily delight in pleasure and mirth,
Always receive the first Fruits of the Earth.
We never are without Pudding or Sauce,
. . . . you Londoners . . . . such a . . .
. . . . labour you . . . . Hot.

The Royal Exchange was given its name by charter in 1571, and *don* was first used to mean a distinguished person in 1634 (*OED*): but the theme, in general terms, was a common one throughout the seventeenth and eighteenth centuries. The last lines are incomplete in the only version we have seen.

102

Riley and Colinband

Printed and Sold by J. Davenport, No. 6, Georges Court,
St. John's Lane, West Smithfield, London

Rise up William Riley come along with me
I mean to go with you and leave this country,
O leave thy fathers dwelling, houses and free land,
Away goes William Riley, and his dear Colinband.

O'er hills and mountains along the lonesome lane,
Thro' groves and vallies bad company to rafrain
Her father he pursu'd her and with a chosen band,
Taken was poor Riley with his Colinband.

Home she was taken and in her closet bound,
Riley he was taken, and put in Sligo goal,
All the toil and slavery I'm willing to stand,
Still hoping to be saved by my dear Colinband.

Now I am in cold irons my hands and feet are bound
Handcuffed like a robber and chain'd to the ground
But all the toil and slavery I am willing to stand;
Still hoping to be saved by my dear Colinband.

Down came the goaler's son and to William did say
Rise, you William Riley, you must appear this day,
To feel squire Fowler's anger quiet you must stand
In hopes to be saved by your dear Colinband.

'Twas but last night I heard these words of thee,
That the lady's oath would hang or set you free,
If that be so, said Riley, her pleasure I will stand,
In hopes to be saved by my dear Colinband.

Ye gentlemen of the jury with pity look on me,
This rascal came among us to disgrace my family,
The impudence of this inferior I am not fit to stand
If I don't see satisfaction I will leave this Irish land.

The lady she spoke out, with tears reply'd she,
The fault is none of Riley's the blame is all on me
I forc'd him for to leave this place and go along with me,
I lov'd him out of measure which proves our destiny.

Out spoke noble Fox at the table he stood by,
Ye gentlemen of the jury, look on this extremity,
To hang a man for love, is it not murder you see,
So take the life of Riley should he leave the country.

Good, my Lord, he stole her jewels and rings,
Her gold watch, her silver buckles, and many precious things,
Which cost me bright guineas more than 500 pounds
And all these things they were on Riley found.

Good my Lord, I gave them as a token of true love
And when that we are parting he will no more remove
If you have them Riley pray send them home to me
I will my loving lady, with many thanks to thee.

There is one ring among them that yourself may wear
With thirty locket of diamonds well set in silver fair
                                        [?the pretty locket
There is a token of true love with it on your right hand,   [?wear
That you are mine, and my heart is broke when you're in some
    foreign land,

Out spoke noble Fox you may let the prisoner go,
The lady's oath is clear, the jury all my know,   [may
She has releas'd her own true love, has renewed his name,
For her honour great might gain an estate as ever rose to fame.

'Colinband' probably = Irish cuilin bán, fair girl. For a melody, and further
details, see Journal of the English Folk-Song Society, vol. III (1908-9), pp.
133-6, where the events described in the ballad are mentioned as having
occurred c. 1800. W. Joyce, Old Irish Folk Music and Song (1909), p. 230,
locates the events of this ballad in the vicinity of Bundoran, near Sligo, in
the late eighteenth century, and gives 'Squire Fowler's' real name as
ffolliott.

103

The Rolling Kiddy

The youth comes up to town to learn all modern foppery,
To London town, no better place to teach those from the country,
He soon finds out what is wanting, like him he sees one in ten,
He runs to the barber's shop and gets a swinging tail, and then,
O this is the way to be a rolling Kiddy O,
The girls will admire you, and say you are the tippy O.

He learneth for to fight, gets drunk a quarrel to begin,
And goes with the Garden lads to every night bawdy ken,
He is to call with authority and not lose his consequence,
To knock down the glasses and make no recompence.
For now he is made compleat, etc.

Like his new companions the blowings he is to try to bilk,
And if they will not stand the lunge he is to kick the fancy jilt,
And say he is a man of independent property,
And wonders at their impudence so ill to treat his company,
For now he is made, etc.

Here he takes the best advice, his money it growing low,
Like those upon the roads, who for the cash a thieving go,
Great is the danger, yet shews a man of courage bold,
For life or death, but never be without the gold,
For now he is made, etc.

At hazard quite the knowing one, what is got may quickly fly,
At the ensuing dark moon to get a fresh supply,
But if the traps should hobble him, why then he is sent to quod,
Great George he may pardon him, one more to strut abroad.

[?once

But if the saucy blowing shou'd nap the sure reward,
While he is by a brother pad hanging by the fatal cord,
No more he is complete a rolling Kiddy O,
The morning dilly puts a stop to such a rolling tippy O.

The Rolling Kiddy, 'the smart thief'; cf. *Partridge* (1), who gives *ca.* 1820–90 for the expression. *Great George*, however, indicates a date before 1830. *the tippy*, the height of fashion. *the Garden*, Covent Garden. *ken*, house. *call with authority*, for drink. *blowings*, fast women. *trap*, an officer. *dilly* (= diligence), coach, here probably the hangman's cart, though *OED* does not record this sense before 1850. In spite of the above dates, this piece may well be eighteenth-century. For the block, cf. nos 5 and 6. Evans probably printed the version given here.

104

The Rover

When I was a wild and rambling boy,
Always in the alehouse boozing,
The landlord he prov'd kind to me,
The gallows old whore was always a growling.

The landlord he went out one day,
Left me in the alehouse bawling,
Three virgins they came flocking in,
Surrounding me like bees a swarming.

One of them was kinder than the rest,
She was one of my own chusing,
I clapt my hand below her waist,
And caught her by her band of Music.

I went up stairs unto my bed,
The chamber door was open,
Now, said I, it is my time,
To shut all doors that I find open.

I pull'd my shoes from off my feet,
And gently stept into the chamber,
With kisses sweet and compliment,
Have you any lodging for a stranger?

The fair maid made me this reply,
I fear young man you are a Rover,
The Devil a word this young man said,
But cry'd my dear, lie further over.

He instantly jumpt into bed,
And immediately threw his leg over,
The Devil a word this fair maid said,
But lay and laugh'd till the game was over.

Then I heard a d—— noise,
Who should it be but her mother,
Caught me between her daughter's thighs;
The gallows old whore sung out murder.

She said, young man, my daughter you smother,
Your daughter I will surely wed,
Provided I could get no other,
Then nimbly jumped out of bed.

He caught her by the gallows old shoulder,
And shov'd her head behind the door,
And left her there to curse her daughter,
For all that had happen'd to her before.

The abrupt transitions between 'I' and 'he' much enliven this piece, but
scarcely argue in favour of its being a duet. *Rover*, male flirt, recorded in
OED to 1721 only, but *OED* and Partridge (1) both give the adjectival
use of 'gallows', as here, only for the late eighteenth century on.

105

The Sailor's Frolick

A New Song

One night I came on shore with my pockets lin'd with gold,
And walking thro' the city, a Madam brisk and bold,
Drest in her furbelows, that was her cunning trick,
The crafty jade she smiling said, How goes it cousin Dick.

I stared at my kinswoman, seeing her drest so fine,
I ask'd her then to go and a drink a glass or two of wine,
She took me at my word, like a Town-Miss well bred,
Then madam she grew fond of me, and call'd me Cousin Ned.

We went unto a tavern, and call'd for an upper room,
The drawer stood amaz'd, she in her sweet perfume,
And I in pitch and tar, which much amaz'd the man,
But madam she grew great with me, and call'd me Cousin John.

No sooner was she set, but madam she began to call,
For white wine and canary, poor Jack must pay for all;
Drawer pray be quick, see that you watch and fill,
Let's have a quart of every sort, what say'st thou Cousin Will.

I gave her my consent, and the liquor it came up,
My Miss and I together drank a hearty cup,
We drank a hearty cup, but pray good friends behold
All that the whore wanted of me was to bilk me of my gold.

Down in my pockets deep I catch'd her nimble hand,
A searching for my money as you shall understand,
I rose up in a rage, and little said but mum,
Then round the room I did presume to kick my cousin's bum.

Must I that sails the seas where the stormy winds do blow
And tossed about by billows, be thus affronted, No:
I'll maul you first, and then your furbelows I'll tear,
And then at length with all my strength I'll kick you down the
    stairs.

This frigate must be rigg'd, and friends to tell you plain
She must have new rigging before she sails again;
I watch'd her as she run, she look'd distrest and mean,
And her streaming flags flew all in rags, the like was never seen.

O then I call my landlord, and strait I paid my shot,
And the thoughts of my new kinswoman shall never be forgot;
I wish all were serv'd so, that ever strives to mar,
A sailor bold, or bilk the gold of a jolly valiant Tar.

Probably eighteenth-century. Variations on the general theme, and also
its converse (the sailor duped by a fast woman) are extremely numerous.

106

The Sailor's Happy Marriage

There was an old merchant of honor and fame,
He lived in London, I knew not his name,
He had a young daughter, whose beauty was clear,
And persons of honour did court her we hear.

Yet nevertheless she refused them all,
And lov'd a young sailor that was proper and tall,
She sent him a letter, her mind to reveal,
That she was not able her love to conceal.

He received the letter with great joy and mirth,
And unto her father he presently went:
There unto each other revealed their minds,   [?They
With many sweet kisses and compliments fine.

At last her old father got word by the bye,
That on the young sailor she had cast an eye;
Ne'er mind, said her father, I will them soon part.
I'll seem to prove kind, tho' 'tis not in my heart.

Next morning as soon as the stairs he came down,
He call'd on his daughter, they say with a frown;
Saying beautiful daughter will you speak and embrace,
And marry a sailor, your friends to disgrace.

Dear honored father, your pardon I crave,
There is none in the world but the sailor I'll have;
For he is my dear, and my only joy,
And if I don't have him, myself I'll destroy.

Well beautiful daughter, if it is your lot,
To marry a sailor I'll hinder you not;
But pray do it in private, talk nothing of me,
And when it is over we'll bravely agree.

But when they were going in at the church door,
A press-gang did meet them, 'twas near to a score;
Instead of being married, he was pressed away,
So nothing was there but a sorrowful day.

This fair maid she dressed herself up in mens clothes,
And unto the very same captain she goes;
She entered herself, and it fell to her lot,
To lay in her love's arms, tho' he knew not.

When many a night with each other they had laid
And many a night with each other had sail'd;
O! once I'd a true love, the sailor did say,
But her cruel parents they press'd me away.

'Tis very well known I was brought up to my pen,
Some knowledge and 'strolage, I act now and then,
Come tell me your age, and I'll throw up your lot,
And tell whether you'll ever have her or not.

Then straight in her arms like lightening he flew
Saying, many a hazard I've ventured for you;
You might see how the sailor enjoy'd his sweetheart,
No doubt but the sailor could act his own part.

Now when the couple return'd to this land,
Her father was dead as we understand;
And she was heiress of her father's estate,
And he was the Lord of riches most great.

Now this couple was married, as plainly appears,
Enjoying one another without dread or fears;
With love out of measure, unto their content,
And spendeth their lives in sweet innocence.

Eighteenth-century. The block suggests a stage setting, but the ballad is in the popular as against the concert tradition; the confused transitions seem not to detract from the life and vividness of this piece. *'strolage*, astrology?

107

Sally Mac Gee

You sporting young girls, give ear to my ditty,
Pray listen a while you may smile at the same
I'm a buxom young girl just come from the city,
I love for to play at young Venus's game;
I sport and carouse in jovial meriment,
With buxom young rakes of every degree,
In drinking and carousing is all my element,
I am the girl called Sally Mac Gee.

When forced from the town I came to the country
I met a young Draper, who did me salute,
He lovingly embraced me, and shew'd his gallantry,
With plenty of liquors and money to boot,
The night being come to sport we went merrily,
And while we were playing I sure did make free,
His pockets did plunder of guineas in number,
Which makes him to think of Sally M'Gee:

The next was a lawyer, and with law attornies,
Came bowing and scraping, and making quite free,
With fifty bright shiners in good ready rhinos,
He down on the table did tender to me;
I gave him diversion, and pleased him quite heartily,
Right willingly he paid me a double fee,
I scorch'd his quil with the coal of curiosity,
Which makes him to think on young Sally M'Gee.

The next was a miser, who thought himself wiser,
Than all the whole world, so griping was he;
His bags he did open, and as a love token,
A two hundred pound note he give unto me;
I gave diversion, and pleas'd him quite heartily,
I surely did please him, and that to a tee,
I gave him the slip, and a smoking hot pip,
Now run to the doctor, says Sally M'Gee.

The next was an alefeller with a wife and fortune,
Who had set up that business two years or three,
With fifty bright shiners he came on to court me;
And his fortune he left it with me,
But I thought it pity to wrong wife and children,
Within my breast I did quickly agree,
I sent her the booty, word how I came by it,
Which makes her right thankful to Sally M'Gee.

The next was a farmer, and he was a charmer,
And then with his person I did quickly agree,
I liked well his courage, and joined him in marriage,
And ever right constant to him I will be;
Fifty bright pounds I got in my rounds,
I gave for a portion, so pleasing was he,
I live in the county Tyrone, tis very well known,
More luck and good fortune to Sally M'Gee.

Irish, as is clear from the rhyme-scheme and polysyllables as well as the reference to Co. Tyrone; but 'Printed and Sold at 21, East Smithfield' (i.e. J. Thompson). *rhino*, cash (*OED*, 1688). *pip*, syphilis, *Partridge* (1) gives 'late c. 16–17'; but almost certainly eighteenth-century here.

108

Saw you My Father

A Favourite Scotch Song

Saw you my father,
Saw you my mother,
Saw you my true love John;
He told his only dear,
That he soon would be here,
But he to another is gone.

I saw not your father,
I saw not your Mother,
But I saw you true love John;   [your
He has met with some delay,
Which has caused him to stay,
But he will be here anon.

244

Then John he up arose.
And to the door he goes.
And he twirled, he twirled at the pin;
The Lassie took the hint,
And to the door she went,
And she let her true love in.

Fly up, Fly up,
My boney Grey Cock,
And crow when it is day;
Your breast shall be,
Of the beaming Gold,
And your Wing of the Silver Grey.

The Cock he proved false,
And untrue he was,
For he crowed an hour too soon;
The Lassie thought it day,
So she sent her love away,
And it prov'd by the blink of the moon. [but the

boney, bonny. For a melody to this beautiful piece see P. W. Joyce, *Old Irish Folk Music and Songs*, Dublin, 1909, II, p. 731.

109

Scew Ball

[Sold at No. 42, Long Lane]

Come gentlemen sportsmen I pray listen all,
I will sing you a song in praise of Scew Ball,
And how he came over you shall understand,
It was by Squire Merwin the pearl of our land.

And of all his late actions that I've heard before,
He was lately challeng'd by one Sir Ralph Gore,
For five hundred guineas on the plains of Kildare,
To run with Miss Sportly, that charming grey mare.

Scew Ball he then hearing the wager was laid,
Unto his kind master said, don't be afraid,
For if on my side you thousands lay would,
I will rig in your castle a fine mass of gold.

The day being come, and the cattle walk'd forth,
The people came flocking from East, North, and South,
For to view all the sporters, as I do declare,
And venture their money all on the grey mare.

Squire Mirwin then smiling unto them did say,
Come gentlemen all that's got money to lay,
And you that have hundreds, come I'll lay you all.
For I will venture thousands on famous Scew Ball.

Squire Merwin then smil'd, and thus he did say,
Come gentlemen sportsmen, to-morrow's the day,
Your horses and saddles and bridles prepare,
For we must away to the plains of Kildare.

The day being come, and the cattle walk'd out,
Squire Mirwin he order'd his rider to mount,
And all the spectators for to clear the way,
The time being come, not one moment delay.

These cattle were mounted, and away they did fly,
Scew Ball like an arrow past Miss Sportly by,
The people went up for to see them go round,
They said in their hearts that they ne'er touch'd the ground.

But as they were running, in the midst of the sport,
Squire Mirwin to his rider began this discourse,
O loving kind rider come tell unto me,
How far is Miss Sportly this moment from thee?

O loving kind master you bear a great stile,
The grey mare's behind me a long English mile,
If the saddle maintains, I'll warrant you there,
You ne'er will be beat on the plains of Kildare.

But as they were running by the distance chair,
The gentlemen cry'd out, Scew Ball never fear,
Altho' in this country thou wast ne'er seen before,
Thou has beaten Miss Sportly, and broke Sir Ralph Gore.

Scew Ball, skewbald (cf. piebald). An Irish ballad, reproduced here from a London printing. *cattle*, horses. *rider* in stanza 9 appears to mean 'mount' (cf. scooter). *North, and South*, l.14, should probably read 'South and North' for the rhyme.

I IO

The Servant's Pedigree

Davenport, Printer, George's Court, Clerkenwell.

At the butler and housekeeper I shall begin,
From a charity-school their education bring,
Why, you rogue and saucy jade, how dare you speak to me?
Hackball himself could not tell your pedigree.

It is of the cook's postillion—I mean a kitchen-maid,
Of a cook's pantry, I've often heard it said,
For to take her in the dark and show her what is right,
The new and true way to keep her spit bright.

As for a greasy cook she's often in a pet,
Grudging the poor kitchen-girl what she could get;
But we will tip her the cordial, and take her in the gig,
She will pawn cloak and kitchen-stuff to dust her perriwig.

The housemaid she comes down in her bedgown and shift,
For to get in her favour you must give her a lift,
Dry-rub her rooms, ne'er a tale will she tell,
Clap her hands on your pop's head, and dust her ceiling well.

There is a nurse in the house that has the worst of bad luck,
We dare not say a word for the spoiling of her suck,
When the new-milk days are over we'll take her out to grass,
We'll pay off the old score with kicks upon her a——.

If her whipper-in be saucy, or sets up her snout,
We dare not say ill she did, while washing of her clouts,
But will take her by the two heels and dip her in the suds,
And will have her there bathing with little master's duds.

See the pretty dairy-maid, how she trips it along the field,
With a pail upon her arm, to see what the cow doth yield,
Lost herself in the meadow, I cannot tell you how,
They said she milk'd the bull, my boys, before she milk'd the cow.

As for our coachman, he looks very big,
With his three-cock'd hat and his three-curl'd wig,
With his long-quarter'd shoes buckl'd down to his toe
With his whip in his hand, he's a tiptoe glado.

As for the lady's footman, he goes before the chair,
With his fine ruffl'd shirt and his well-powder'd hair,
Stand about, clear, as if the streets were his own,
Tho' there's ne'er a border on his mammy's cap at home.

Eighteenth-century, from many details. *dry-rub*, to beat severely (*Partridge* (1), seventeenth to eighteenth century). *pop*, pistol: here clearly metaphorical. *tiptoe glado*, probably gipsy slang, not in *Partridge* (1).

III

The Sheffield Prentice

I was brought up at Sheffield, but not of high degree,
My parents doated on me, because they had none but me,
I rode about for pleasure where my fancy led,
Till I was bound apprentice, then all my joys were fled.

I did not like my master, he did not use me well,
I made a resolution not long with him to dwell,
Unknown to my parents I then ran away,
And steer'd my course to London, cursed be the day.

But when I came to London, a Lady met me there,
She offer'd me great wages to serve her one year,
Deluded by her promises, with her I did agree
To go with her to Holland, which prov'd my destiny.

We had not left Old England past years two or three,
Before my young wealthy mistress grew very fond of me,
She said her gold and silver, her house and land,
If I'd consent to have her, should be at my command.

I said, dear loving mistress, I can't wed you both,
For I have already promised, and made a solemn oath,
To wed with Sally, your handsome chambermaid,
Excuse me now, dear mistress, she has my heart betray'd.

My mistress in a passion from me did go,
Protesting when she left me she would work my overthrow,
So much perplext in humour she could not be my wife,
She swore she'd seek a project to take away my life.

As I walk'd in the garden, just at the dawn of day,
My mistress stood a watching the pretty flowers gay,
The ring from off her finger, as I pass'd by,
She slipt into my pocket, and for the same I die.

My mistress swore I robb'd her, and straightway I was brought
Before a cruel Justice, to answer for my fault,
And long I pleaded guiltless, but it was all in vain,
My mistress swore against me, and I was sent to gaol.

And at the last assizes try'd I was and cast,
And then the heavy sentence of death on me was past,
From thence to execution they dragg'd me to the tree,
So God reward my mistress, for she has ruin'd me.

All that stand around me, my cruel fate to see,
Don't glory in my downfal, but pray pity me,
Farewel my dear Sally, I bid this world adieu,
Farewel my dear Sally, I die for serving you.

cast, condemned. For melody (and an abridged version of the text) see
Peggy Seeger and Ewan MacColl, *The Singing Island*, 1961, p. 87, or
Journal of the English Folk-Song Society, vol. I (1899–1904), pp. 200–1, and
vol. II (1905–6), p. 169.

112

The Soldier's Sweetheart

Sold at 15, Long Lane, West Smithfield—where
Shopkeepers and Hawkers may be Supplied

Sweetheart, if I for a Soldier should go,
Sweetheart what would you do then,
If you go for a Soldier, it will make you bolder,
And we'll double it over again.

Sweetheart, if I to the camps should go,
Sweetheart what would you do then,
If you go to the camp it will learn you to scamp,
And we'll double it over again.

Sweetheart, if I for a soldier should go,
Sweetheart what would you do then,
I would call for your pay of a shilling a day,
And we'll double it over again.

Sweetheart if I some money should want,
Sweetheart what would you do then,
Then I'd kiss for a crown with a country crown,   [?clown
And we'll double it over again.

Sweetheart if I should get you with child,
Sweetheart what would you do then,
You must get me another to play with the other,
And double it over again.

Sweetheart if I should chance to die,
Sweetheart what would you do then,
I'd bury you brave, and another soon have,
And double it over again.

Printed after *c.* 1795, since the block shows a medallion inscribed 'République Française—Echange des Prisonniers'. *scamp*, to go out as a highway robber.

113

The Sparrows

Twas in the pleasant month of may,
When males and females sport and play,
A wanton sparrow full of prate,
With spousy on a tree was sat;
They talk'd how faithful they would be,
And chirp'd eternal constancy;
The only thing that damp'd their sport,
Was fear their lives would be too short.

But as from bough to bough they fly,
Not dreaming any creature nigh,
For want of a more downy bed,
Upon a twig with bird lime spread,
In haste their fond regard to prove,
They take their little fill of love:
The only thing that damp'd their sport,
Was fear their lives would prove too short.

But pains to pleasure soon succeed,
To both it prov'd a fatal deed;
For tho' with ease they broke away,
And baulk'd a school boy of his prey;
The bridegroom in the hasty strife,
Was stuck so fast unto his wife,
That tho' they us'd their utmost art,
They quickly found they ne'er must part.

A gloomy cloud o'ercast his brow,
He found himself he knew not how;
He pouts and glouts and peevish grew,
As other angry husbands do:
Whene'er he mov'd, he felt her still,
She kiss'd him oft against his will;
With favours still o'erwhelm'd her lord,
Abroad, at home, at bed, at board.

But he still obstinate and stout,
At length her stock of love was out,
So back to back in discontent,
They sit and sullenly repent.
Thus after some few hearty pray'rs,
A jostle, and some spiteful tears,
This is the burthen of their song,
That life is tedious and too long.

Clearly eighteenth-century in this version (note 'spousy', l.4), though perhaps from an earlier, literary, original. *prate*, prattle. *glout*, frown, look sullen. The tail block on the printing we have used consisted of the words 'Peter Henry: A Chemist', and the block was printed upside-down.

114

The Sunbury Hair Dresser

Sold at No. 15 Long Lane West Smithfield,
Travellers and Country Dealers may be supplied

In Sunbury town as I've heard tell,
There lives a noble barber,
And he was caught the truth to tell,
In a Romanos's larder,
I never learn he had to dress,
In that place ere a wig sir,
But it is said that he had got,
A mind to shave the pig sir.
  Bow wow, etc.

When he got in he look'd all round,
To see what he could find sir.
An unknown hand there chance to be,
That lock'd him in behind sir,
The barber cries pray let me out,
I'm looking for the cat sir,
But he had got his apron on,
And went without his hat sir.

As if he went to shave the pig
That in the salt did lay sir,
Or otherwise his fine address,
To the rib-spare there to pay sir,
But let that be how'ere it will
No matter not a flower,
The barber there, was caught I say,
And kept there for an hour.

At last the door it was unlock'd,
Out march'd Mr. Barber,
To see spectators and to bid
Farewell unto the larder,
And now my song is ore done   [o'er and
I hope yu'll not refuse it,
And if the barber with it meets,
I'm sure he will abuse it.

The metre and refrain suggest that this piece was sung to the same melody as Lewis Carroll later had in mind when writing 'Speak roughly to your little boy . . .' (*Alice's Adventures in Wonderland*).

115

The Tar's Frolic
or, the Adventures of a
British Sailor

Printed and sold by J. Davenport, 6, George's Court,
St. John's Lane, West-Smithfield

Give ear, brother seamen, and listen a while,
I'll sing you a ditty will make you smile,
It's concerning a frolic as I'll to you tell,
As fortune would have it was very well.

My discharge I've now got, and have gold in store,
And soon I will tell you how I added to it more,
I being drunk, to an alehouse went in,
To dance and to caper I then did begin.

Some doxies being there seem'd quite full of glee,
Thinks I to myself there's one of them for me,
One being well rigg'd in a fine long silk gown,
I tip'd her the wink and she by me sat down.

I call'd for the waiter some liquor to bring,
Said the doxy unto me, that is just the thing,
Besides, for my Jack, I'll a lodging provide,
And I'll be the girl that shall lie by your side.

All things being agreed between doxy and I,
I call'd for the waiter to know what's to pay,
Fifteen shillings and sixpence the waiter reply'd,
I pay'd down the money, and up stairs we hied.

I quickly unrigg'd, and jump'd into bed,
I planted my shot locker under my head,
When my doxy and I bid each other good night,
I sham'd fast asleep, and she thought herself right.

Upright in the bed then my doxy arose,
In searching about to find out my clothes,
And quickly after I knew her design,
For all her whole search was to find out my coin.

I jump'd out of bed and I well laid her on,
With a stick I had by me as thick as my thumb.
The smock she had on like ribbons it flew,
She cry'd ten thousand murders and what shall I do.

She danc'd round the room and I follow'd my blows
I gave her no time to put on her clothes,
She open'd the door and down stairs she run,
I fasten'd it after and laugh'd at the fun.

I search'd round the room to see what I could find,
And Moll in the fray left her pockets behind.
With ten guineas in them and two five pound notes,
Moll left this behind with her gown and her coats.

This all being over the morning drew nigh,
And light thro' a window I happen'd to spy.
I ty'd up the treasure and all I had found,
The money, the petticoats, stockings and gown.

Now to conclude and finish my song,
Three guineas I made of coat, stockings and gown,
So we'll laugh at the frolic and drink the health round,
And wish each brother seamen the same in town.

doxy, prostitute. The first and last stanzas suggest that this ballad was
composed with performances aboard ship or in a sailors' pub in mind. The
Blakeian block should be noted. This ballad has recently been collected by
R. S. Thomson from the singing of Mr Harry Cox, Catfield, Norfolk.

116

They'll all Do It
or, Bung your Eye

I am a Country Lad 'tis true,
And it was my Inclination;
To come up to London town,
There to see the Fashion;
But at first I was surpriz'd,
To hear so odd a Cry Sir,
Some call out, will you wheedle away,
And some cry'd, Bung your Eye Sir.
   What they meant, I long'd to know,
Soon they did inform me,
And said it was a Dram or so,
That would both cheer and warm me;
For they said 'twas very good,
To keep out Wind and Weather;
So I sat down among the Rest,
And we Bung'd our Eyes together.
   'tis the Fashion now in town;
And very much in Vogue Sir,
From the Courtier to the Clown,
Each will take his Cogue Sir:
Few there is will it refuse,

Or will the same refuse Sir,
Which if you do discreetly use,
You may safely Bung your Eye Sir.
   Madam that does keep her Coach,
Oftentimes will dose it,
And when she wants a Dram of Nants,
Slips into her Closet,
Because she cares not to be seen,
But does it in private Sir:
And we find 'tis very plain,
She loves to Bung her Eye Sir.
   And the Maid that is coy,
With her pish and fie Sir,
You may gain her Female toy,
If once you Bung her Eye Sir:
Tho' before she seem'd so loath,
To yield up her Charms Sir,
Then you'll find she'll be so kind,
To hug you in her Arms Sir.
   The dissembling whining Saint,
Who will not swear or lye Sir,
When he finds his Spirits faint,
Strait he Bungs his Eye Sir:
Since the Creature is so good,
Why should we it despise Sir;
'Twill nourish and refine your Blood,
Then let us bung our Eye Sir.

Bung your Eye, drink heartily (*Partridge* (1), mid-eighteenth to early nineteenth-century). *Cogue*, a wooden cup. *Nants* (= Nantes), brandy.

262

117

Tippy Jack's Journey to Brighton

Sold at No. 7, Little Catherine Street, Strand
[i.e. Davenport].

Oh! ye bucks and ye bloods o' the town,
    Come listen awhile unto me;
'Tis Jack, oh my Jack so renown'd,
    And that is young Gilpin you see.
'Tis of what did befal t'other day;
    To be sure it was only a rig;
But this I will certainly say,
    It was all along driving my gig!

(SPEAKS)—And as papa Gilpin's journey to Edmonton
has made a bit of noise, I will just give a short
description of my intended trip to Brighton:—You
must know, that my filly, thorough bred, in turning
round the corner of Garlic-hill took fright at the face
of an old clothes-man; and without the least ceremony,
pitched me plump into the centre of a mud-cart, where
I began to sing—
    Ri-um-ti-idity um, etc.

Well, up I was once more again,
    And thanks to my stars too, unhurt;
And when fix'd in my gig look'd the thing,
    Except something worse for the dirt.
My elbows I knowingly squar'd—
    I seem'd like a swallow to fly:
When plump against the post run the mare,
    And down again headlong came I.

(SPEAKS)—Dam'me I was now tossed into a fruit-stall,
where the apples and pears rolled one way, and I
head-over-heels another:—Twig the taylor, says
one—You lie, says another, its the barber. Oh! thank
ye, gentlemen, says I, it's only—
    Ri-um-ti-idity-um, etc.

263

So when the damage was paid,
    Away gallop'd I out of sight;
But scarce had another street made,
    Before she again, Sirs, took fright;
For spanking along Piccadilly,
    I somehow run over a pig.
When off set the bitch of a filly,
    And bundled me out of the gig.

(SPEAKS)—Oh! this was not the worst job of all: for
after I had paid the butcher two pounds, seven shillings
and threepence three-farthings, for the loss of his grunter;
in touching the mare under the left flank, in order to evade
paying the turnpike at Hyde Park-Corner, she run me against
the posts, half-kill'd an old beggar-woman and upset a
man-milliner, smack'd the shafts in two and left me
sprawling in the dirt:—Why don't you get up? says the
turn-pike man:—Why don't you keep moving, Sir? says
another. Damn you, says I, don't you see I'm moving?
So I begun to sing—
    Ri-um-ti-itidy-um, etc.

Probably *c.* 1783, when the Prince Regent moved to Brighton. Cowper's
'John Gilpin' was first published in 1780. *tippy*, smart, fashionable. The
piece is reminiscent of Dibdin's patter-songs, and may be by him.

118

The True Blues of Horsham

Did you ever hear of this new made song,
About Walters and his men being the worst under the sun,
But say what they will I will give them their due,
They are bold hearty fellows like men that will stand true.
    Fire away, cut away.

It would have made you for to smile to see how they act,
When bold Jindon and his men first fell into the track,
He said my boys come on be sure you do not part,
For surely this morning we will make them for to smart.
    Fire away, cut away.

The smugglers they were some distance before,
Two hundred they say, but I'm sure there were more,
'Twas all upon a common where they beset us around,
But we soon made them glad for to quit that spot of ground.
    Fire away, cut away.

Oh! when that we had gain'd their attack,
For to see how hearty and noble they did act,
Clap spurs to our horses and chas'd over the ground, [?their
But we soon made them glad for to quit that spot of ground.
    Fire away, cut away.

But the best of it all we had in their fun,
Old Carey was their captain and he was oblig'd to run,
He got graz'd on his thigh and his money shot away,
He said my boys come on for it will not do to stay.
    For they fire away, cut away.

I hope that you take notice of my song,
For the Smugglers in general are sure to be wrong,
For while they are empty here how they make their brags,
But when they are loaded we are sure to have their bags.
    We fire away, cut away.

So now to conclude and to finish my song,
Mr. Walter is our master and never will see us wrong,
Like a general in battle he says my boys stand true,
Then answereth his men, Sir, we are all True Blue.
　　When we fire away, cut away.

True Blue, faithful (n. or adj.). Apparently an answer to a 'new made song' attacking 'Walters and his men'. The ballad is obscure as regards the names: perhaps 'Jindon' commands a scouting party of revenue-men, and 'Mr. Walter' the whole body.

119

Unfortunate Billy

Tune—Mrs. Casey

When Billy first to London came,
To be the rolling kiddy,
With leather breech, and oaken cane,
He thought himself the tippy;
To cock his glass and tip the wink,
He learnt the genteel nicky,
For while his fob contain'd the chink,
He was the rolling kiddy.

CHORUS

With nine inch stick,
To be the kick,
Repair to London city,
There tip the wink,
Being full of chink,
And roll about your dicky.

To shuffle, cog, and throw a dice,
He soon became the tippy,
With ladies fair to grace his side,
He'd prance about the city;
To break a lamp and beat the watch,
The youth was apt and ready,
For while his pouch contains the cash,
He was the rolling kiddy.

CHORUS

With nine inch stick, etc.

At masquerades, at plays or ball,
Our hero was the kicky,
He'd cock his glass, and view them all,
Then roll about his dicky;
Till leering Nan, and Teddy Blink,
Had stagg'd the knowing laddy,
They nurs'd the cull, and bon'd his chink,
Then sent him home to daddy.

CHORUS

With nine inch stick,
No more the kick,
Farewel to London city,
No more to wink,
For want of chink,
Or roll about his dicky.

kiddy, a flash minor thief. tippy, height of fashion. nippy, smart (fellow). kick, fashion. roll . . . your dickey, drive your donkey (c. 1811). 'Billy' is a flash 'coster'. cog, cheat. stagged, probably 'informed against' (Partridge (1), late 1830s). daddy, probably the workhouse keeper, but possibly the idea is that Billy has to go home to his parents in the country, once his money is spent. The tune 'Mrs. Casey' is also cited for no. 9 ('The Blue Lion'): see also the note to no. 67 ('Landlady Casey').

120

The Unfortunate Citizen:
Or The Comical Robbery

A Citizen for his Recreation's sake,
A Journey in the Country he would take,
Who drinking of Healths and shaking Hands also,
As if to some new-found Land he would go.

He had not rid not passing Miles half a score,
But upon the Road he met with Four
Who bid him stand and his Purse deliver,
For we are the takers and you must be the giver.

Then into the Wood they haled him in,
And there they stripped him unto the skin,
I pray kind Gentlemen some favour to me show;
For in riffling me you rob you know not who.

This Horse I ride on indeed 'tis my Brothers;
My Coat that I wear I borrow'd of another.
My boots I had of a Grocer in the Strand,
And the Spurs I borrow'd of a Serving Man.

This Beaver Hat I borrow'd of a Sailor.
My Swash and Breeches I borrow'd of a Taylor,
My Saddle, Doublet, and fine silken Hose,
They're our Church-Wardens all the Parish know

This Ring I have on that has this precious stone
I borrow'd it of my dear Cousin Joan,
Her Husband does not know it kind Gentlemen,
This is the Case I pray show Favour then.

Then reply'd the Thieves what need you care,
When in your Loss so many bears a share,
Go tell them at London that you met with Four,
And in riffling you they robb'd half a score.

121

The Valiant Welshman

Tune—Ram of Derby

There was a jovial Welshman,
　　As I have heard many say;
And he came up to London
　　Upon St. David's-day.

With a wooden sword, sir, by his side,
　　And a leek stuch in his crown,
Mounted upon a nanny goat,
　　Hur rides to London town.

And as hur was strutting along, sir,
  As great as any king,
Poor Taffy happen'd to meet, sir,
  With a swinging great Pressgang.

What ship? then says the sailors,
  Come you must serve the king:
Cot-splutter a-nails, says the Welshman,
  Sir, hur is a shentleman.

Hur will not fight by land, sir,
  Nor hur will not fight by sea;
Prithee let her go, sir,
  What wants the king with me?

Come you must go to Gibraltar,
  To fight with cannon-ball:
Then Taffy pull'd out his wooden sword,
  And swore he'd kill them all.

Hur is a king herself, sir,
  Upon St. David's-day;
And hur has a house and land, sir:
  Hur's not to be press'd away.

Hur dwells upon a mountain,
  Hur house one story high;
Hur keeps a coat to ride upon,
  And a pig, sir, in hur sty.

Hur's got a house well furnish'd,
  With the best of good Welsh ware,
A spoon, and a wooden chamber-pot,
  My grandmother's leather chair.

Hur's got a cage to keep a bird,
  And a cat to catch a mouse;
Besides, sir, like a shentleman,
  A dog to keep her house.

And if you do press such shentlemen,
  I think it is not right:
Besides, you may tell the King, sir,
  He may go himself to fight.

The lieutenant he laugh'd aloud,
　　To hear what he did say:
But they press'd this good shentleman,
　　And sent him strait to sea.

And when they come to Gibraltar,
　　We make but little doubt,
But Taffy's wooden sword will put
　　The French men to the rout.

And if the French men do come near,
　　And things do happen right,
No doubt but Taffy plays his part,
　　And bravely stands to fight.

The block is perhaps meant to show a Welshman, with a leek in his hat.
Many tunes have been collected with the 'Ram of Derby'.

The Wars are not Over

As I was travelling the country up and down,
Until that I came to a little market-town,
The drums beat loud for soldiers I am sure,
Which made me conclude the Wars were not o'er.

Then in comes the Tanner, and thus he does say:
I have trusted all my leather to a Shoemaker this day,
He's gone for a soldier, which grieveth me full sore,
And he will pay me for my leather when the wars are all o'er.

The next is the Taylor, and thus he does say:
They have knocked down my wages to sixpence a day
The people wear their old cloaths they are grown so poor,
And they will not get new till the wars are all o'er.

Then in come the Barber with razor and ball,
Do you want to be shav'd, kind gentlemen all?
The people wear their old wigs, they are grown so poor,
And they will not get new till the wars are all o'er.

The next trade is the Cooper his trade is good for nought,
His hoops are too long and his staves are too short,
'Tis on the long settle there stands a long score,
And he will not rub it out till the wars are all o'er.

The next is the Blacksmith, his trade is worst of all,
He's sold his bed from under him for iron and coal,
He's taken up his lodgings upon the cold floor,
And there he must remain till the Wars be all o'er.

Then in comes the landlady so neat and so trim,
With her ruffles at her elbows, and thus she does begin,
I've let all my ale go, 'tis for an old score,
And I will pay my maltster when the Wars are all o'er.

Then in came the Devil with the malt on his back,
With anger he stuff'd her in the mouth of his sack,
He took away the landlady, 'tis for an old score,
And he will bring her back again when the Wars are all o'er.

Typical late eighteenth-century sentiments. The block shows a man
apparently singing in the open air with his hat held out as if for money:
the background shows a country church, etc. (cf. stanza 1). *old, long score,*
the customer's indebtedness, recorded (e.g.) by a 'score' on the settle. Reproduced, with another block, in Shepard, *The Broadside Ballad,* p. 143.

123

The Weaver and his Sweetheart

I am a Weaver by my trade,
I fell in love with a servant maid,
If I her favour could but win,
Then I shall weave, and she shall spin.

His father to him scornfully said,
How can you fancy a servant maid,
When you may have ladies fine and gay,
Drest like unto the Queen of May.

As for your ladies I don't care,
Could I but enjoy my only dear,
It makes me mourn when I thought to smile,
And I will wander the woods so wild.

I went unto my love's chamber-door,
Where oftimes I had been before;
But I could not speak nor yet go in,
To the pleasant bed my love lay in.

How can you tell what a pleasant bed,
Where nothing lies but a servant-maid?
A servant-maid altho' she be,
Blest is the man that enjoyeth she.

A pleasant thought came in my mind,
I turned down the sheets so fine,
There I saw two white breasts hang so low
Much like two white hills covered with snow.

My love she lives in the country of North,
And I myself live a great way off;
And when I weave in the county of Down,
Then I will weave her a holland Gown.

My love is sick and like to die,
A most unhappy young man am I;
But at length the Weavers joy was blest,
And he got the servant Maid at last.

The head-block suggests a theatrical setting, though one apparently un-
connected with the song. The tail-block was printed upside-down in the
original. Irish.

124

Wholsome Advice to the Swinish Multitude

A New Song. Tune—Mind, hussy, what you do.

You lower class of human race, you working part I mean,
How dare you so audacious be to read the works of Pain,
The Rights of Man—that cursed book—which such confusion
   brings,
You'd better learn the art of war, and fight for George our King.

      CHORUS

      But you must delve in politics, how dare you thus intrude,
      Full well you do deserve the name of swinish multitude.

There's the laborer and mechanic too, the cobler in his stall,
Forsooth must read the Rights of Man, and Common Sense and
   all!
For shame, I desire ye wretched crew don't be such meddling fools,
But be contented in your sphere, and mind King Charles's rules.

      But you must delve, etc.

He says you've rights like other men, and you do him believe,
But if you will attention give, I'll soon you undeceive,
I'll soon convince you what's your rights, if you're not quite
   insane,
I will in spite of that miscreant, that incendiary, Tom Pain.

      Who has fill'd your head with politics, etc.

If you had your right you'd punish'd be for daring to complain,
Much more to read pernicious books, and I will tell you plain,
It is your right to slave and drudge, deny it if you can,
And thankful be to our good King, you have the name of man.

      But you must delve, etc.

Altho' our good and gracious King so condescending is,
To grant to you, ye base-born crew, a privilege like this;
Because a trifling tax you pay, you murmur and complain,
Don't he protect you from the French?—yes—or else you would
    be slain.

       But you must delve, etc.

He's the Defender of the Faith—most sacred is his name,
Pray did not he proclaim a fast?—your faces hide for shame,
Was it for sins that he had done?—no—surely no such thing,
To fast and pray for a whole day—Lord, what a gracious King.

       But you must delve, etc.

Altho' its from our gracious king that all these blessings flow,
Altho' you sing you need no king, because Pain told you so;
But Reformation's all your cry—and if you keep this rout,
Then you shall have the rights of swine—that's a ring within your
    snout.

       But you must delve, etc.

I pray be wise, and don't despise this kind advice of mine,
Your name regain, and not retain the filthy name of swine;
Let Government do what they please, then you'll be free from
    harm,
For when a Constitution's pure—what needs there a reform.

       So no more delve in politics, no longer thus intrude,
       And not incur that filthy name of Swinish Multitude.

Dated 1795 in an early annotation. The title is taken from Burke's 'Learning will be cast into the mire, and trodden down under the hoofs of a swinish multitude' in his *Reflections on the French Revolution* (1790). The 'Common Sense' in Stanza 2 was the title of a pamphlet of Tom Paine (1766).

125

The Wonder

[Sold at No. 42, Long Lane]
Printed in April, 1794

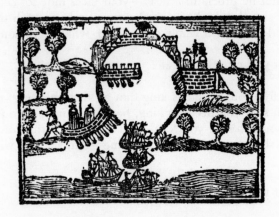

I Wonder, wonder who first invented ships to swim,
To cross the ocean to and fro, what a happy man was him,
He might be call'd some Goddess, like those we have in Spain,
And by his ingenuity in crossing o'er the main.

How should we ever know that there had been foreign lands,
When East India spices are brought ashore, and gold from foreign
   land,
To Virginia for tobacco, up the Streights for sparkling wine,
To Old England for young lasses that go so neat and fine.

It is round and round the globe, my boys, to every port we steer,
Some ships are going up the Streights, some to the India shore,
We pass by dismal mountains, where monstrous fishes swim,
The honour of our Lord above, likewise along the main.

What is a sight more pleasant, to see our well spread sails,
With all the streamers a playing, boys, blest with a pleasant gale,
Extending on the ocean, where mermaids play and sing,
When our ship sails in promotion, to honour George our King.

Sometimes we meet with hurricanes, sometimes with dreadful
  storms,
While death approaches round us in a most dreadful form,
While we all hands are doing the very best we can,
To keep our ship from foundering, and to bring her safe to land.

And when we get all on the Thames, and floating with the tide,
And every jolly sailor bold in their swaggering boats they ride,
There is William calls for Susan, and Tom for buxom Kate,
And every jolly sailor bold enjoys his lovely mate.

The owner of our ship and freight is not half so blest as we,
They do gain their riches, boys, while we are on the seas,
Was it not for seamen bold, Old England would be for ever poor,
For when their money is gone and spent, we will boldly sail for
  more.

The title-word is balanced between its two meanings (marvel, speculation).
A curiously literary-yet-illiterate piece, probably composed before the war
had broken out. The block may be a schematic representation of an
identifiable harbour.

126

World Turn'd Upside Down

When I left the cot of my dad,
    And trudged up to London town,
I thought the folks there wur all mad,
    And the world was turn'd upside down.
One cried ah! how do you do,
    And another stand out of the way.
And they pushed and shoved me about,
    And then cried that's the time of day.
        Tol de lol lol lol lol,
            I'll tell father when I go whoam,
        The folks in London are mad,
            And the world's turn'd upside down.

A soldier came strutting along,
    Drest in clothes so gallant and fine,
Thinks I this a captain must be,
    For Lord how his clothes they did shine
Who should't be but cousin Dick,
    Who left the plough-tail t'other day,
Says I I'll be a soldier to morrow,
    If so be that's the time of day.

But for bargains in London I'm sure,
    You never can be at a loss,
Shopkeepers, so good and so kind,
    Sells all their goods under prime cost,
But when the goods they are all gone,
    They bankrupts become the next day,
And one shilling they pay in the pound,
    Yes and that's the time of day.

Now my myther at home when dress'd,
    Wears four petticoats, large and small,
But the fine ladies now look I vow,
    As if they wore no coats at all,
Then the men they wear womens stays,
    All laced up so fine and so gay,
And women they wear men's breeches,
    O fy—but that's the time of day.

Now while I stood gaping about,
    Where there was row and a racket,
I felt sommat warm in my fob,
    'Twas a man's hand in my pocket,
Says I, sir you've made a mistake,
    Then my gentleman sneaked away
And with all the money I had,
    Yes, and besides my time of day.

I saw over a fine shop door
    Pawnbroker and money lent
I ax'd'em to lend me a crown,
    For my money wer all gone and spent
When he found I'd nothing to pawn,
    Says he you bumpkin walk away,
For we don't lend our money to fools,
    No no, that's not the time of day.

Thinks I it's time to go whoam
    If these are the rigs of the town,
And this is the way the folks serve
    A poor simple and country clown,
What have you seen cry'd myther
    Boy, and what have you got to say,
Why Lunnon myther, is the devil,
    And, myther, that's the time of day.

Partridge (1) gives this use of 'the time of day' as from 1820.

127

The Young Man's Fortune

A New Song

O when I was a young man my valor for to try
O then upon Bow steple I mounted myself high,
My head it hung to westminster my heels was hanging Down,
From thence I jumpt to Dover and never touch'd the Ground,
    Toll, etc.

From thence unto New-castle, and back all in an hour,
From thence I jumpt to London and I mounted on the Tower,
I laid down to sleep Sir, and before I waked again,
O they had hauled me through Italy, through Germany and Spain,
    Tol, etc.

Now I have told you of my projects which I have done of Late,
Now I will Declare to you some of my wealth and Estate,
O I had a little Hen Sir, of her I took great care,
I sett on a muscle shell, and she brought forth a Hare.   [?her

This hare became a mare sir twas full Fourteen hands high,
It was as fine a mare sir as ever was seen with eye,
But now away she is gone in to the north country
And he that will not believe this he may go there and See,
   Tol, etc.

But the worst project which e'er I playd in my life
Was when I made an ugly jump and got me a Wife,
But he that can tell me how to jump from that again,
Sure I will give him my whole Estate likewise my little Hen.

Select Bibliography

This bibliography does not pretend to exhaustiveness, but is virtually confined to those works to which reference is made in the body of the book, or which we have found specifically useful in its preparation. We have omitted a number of items which would more appropriately appear in the bibliographies in later volumes in this series. Place of publication is London unless otherwise indicated.

REFERENCE WORKS

The British Union-Catalogue of Early Music Printed Before the Year 1801, ed. E. D. Schnapper, 2 vols, 1957.

Brown, P. A. H., 'London Publishers and Printers: a Tentative List, *c.* 1800–70', British Museum, typescript, privately issued, 1961.

Crawford, J. L., *Catalogue of a Collection of English Ballads of the Seventeenth and Eighteenth Centuries*, 2 vols, 1890; reprinted New York, 1963.

Crawford, J. L., and Edmond, J. P., *Catalogue of English Broadsides, Fifteen Five to Eighteen Ninety Seven*, 1898; reprinted New York, 1965.

Farmer, J. S., and Henley, W. E., *Slang and its Analogues*, 7 vols, 1890–1904.

Grose, Francis, *A Classical Dictionary of the Vulgar Tongue*, ed. E. Partridge, 1931.

Harben, H. A., *A Dictionary of London*, 1918.

Hodson, W. H., *Hodson's Booksellers', Publishers', and Stationers' Directory for London and Country*, 1855.

Humphreys, A. L., *A Handbook to County Bibliography*, 1917.

Kidson, Frank, 'A bibliography of Dibdin's works', *Notes and Queries*, 1901–4.

The Oxford Dictionary of English Proverbs, ed. W. G. Smith, revised Sir Paul Harvey, 2nd ed., 1948. Referred to as *ODEP*.

The Oxford Dictionary of Nursery Rhymes, ed. Iona and Peter Opie, 1951.

The Oxford English Dictionary, ed. J. A. H. Murray *et al.*, 13 vols, 1933. Referred to as *OED*.

Partridge, Eric (1), *A Dictionary of Slang and Unconventional English*, 2 vols, 7th ed., with revised supplement, 1970.

Partridge, Eric (2), *A Dictionary of the Underworld: British and American*, 3rd ed., 1968.

Partridge, Eric (3), *Slang, To-day and Yesterday*, 4th ed., 1970.

Plomer, H. R., Bushwell, G. H., and Dix, E. R. McL., *Dictionary of Printers and Booksellers, 1726–75,* 1932, with additions in *Durham Philobiblion,* 1950.

Rollins, H. E., *An Analytical Index to the Ballad-Entries, 1557–1709, in the Registers of the Company of Stationers of London,* Durham, North Carolina, 1924; reprinted Detroit, 1966.

Timperley, C. H., *A Dictionary of Printers,* 1839.

Vaux, J. H., *Memoirs . . . including his Vocabulary of the Flash Language,* ed. N. McLachlan, 1964.

Wright, Joseph, *The English Dialect Dictionary,* 6 vols, 1898–1904; reprinted, 1970.

COLLECTIONS AND ANTHOLOGIES

Entries are for the most part made under the name of the editor or compiler; standard ballad collections usually referred to by title are entered under title.

Ashton, J. A., *A Century of Ballads,* 1887; reprinted Detroit, 1968.

Ashton, J. A., *Modern Street Ballads,* 1888.

Ashton, J. A., *Real Sailor Songs,* 1891.

The Bagford Ballads, ed. J. W. Ebsworth, 4 parts, 1878; reprinted New York, 2 vols, n.d.

Bronson, B. H., *The Traditional Tunes of the Child Ballads, with their Texts,* 4 vols, Princeton, 1959–72.

Bronson, B. H., *The Ballad as Song,* Princeton, 1969.

Burns, Robert, *Merry Muses of Caledonia, c. 1800,* ed. James Barke and Sydney Goodsir Smith, 1965.

Child, F. J., *English and Scottish Ballads,* 8 vols, 1861.

Child, F. J., *English and Scottish Popular Ballads,* 10 parts, 1882–98; reprinted New York, 5 vols, 1957.

D'Urfey, Thomas, *Wit and Mirth or Pills to Purge Melancholy,* 1699–1714; expanded and rearranged as *Songs Compleat, Pleasant and Divertive,* 6 vols, 1719–20; facsimile reprints, 1876; New York, 3 vols, 1959.

Farmer, J. S., *Merry Songs and Ballads,* 5 vols, privately printed, 1897.

Farmer, J. S., *Musa Pedestris: Three Centuries of Canting Songs and Slang Rhymes,* privately printed, 1896.

Firth, C. H., *Naval Songs and Ballads,* 1908.

Flanders, H. H., *Ancient Ballads Traditionally Sung in New England* [correlated with the numbered Child collection], Philadelphia, 4 vols, 1960–5.

Furnivall, F. J., and Morfil, W. R., *Ballads from Manuscripts,* 2 vols, 1868, 1873.

Graves, Robert, *English and Scottish Ballads,* 1957.

Healy, J. N., *Ballads from the Pubs of Ireland,* Cork, 1965, 2nd ed., 1966.

Healy, J. N., *The Mercier Book of Old Irish Sreet Ballads,* Cork, 4 vols, 1967–9.

Healy, J. N., *The Second Book of Irish Ballads,* Cork, 1962, 2nd ed., 1964.

Hodgart, M. J. C., *The Faber Book of Ballads,* 1965.

Joyce, P. W., *Old Irish Folk Music and Songs,* Dublin, 1909.

Kidson, Frank, and Moffat, A., *A Garland of English Folk-Song*, 1926.

Lawson, C. C. P., *Naval Ballads and Sea Songs*, intro. C. N. Robinson, 1933.

Logan, W. H., *A Pedlar's Pack of Ballads and Songs*, Edinburgh, 1869.

O'Keeffe, Daniel, *The First Book of Irish Ballads*, Cork, 1955, 4th ed., 1965.

O'Lochlainn, Colm, *Irish Street Ballads*, Dublin, 1939.

O'Lochlainn, Colm, *More Irish Street Ballads*, Dublin, 1965.

The Oxford Book of Ballads, ed. A. Quiller-Couch, 1910; newly selected and edited [including melodies] by James Kinsley, 1969.

The Pepys Ballads, ed. H. E. Rollins, Cambridge, Mass., 8 vols, 1929–32.

Pinto, V. de Sola and Rodway, A. E., *The Common Muse: an Anthology of Popular British Ballad Poetry XVth–XXth Century*, 1957.

Reeves, James, *The Everlasting Circle*, 1960.

Reeves, James, *The Idiom of the People*, 1958.

The Roxburghe Ballads, ed. W. Chappell and J. W. Ebsworth, 8 vols, 1869–99; reprinted New York, 1967.

Seeger, Peggy, and MacColl, Ewan, *The Singing Island*, London and New York, 1961.

Seeman, Erich, *European Folk Ballads*, Copenhagen, 1967.

Sidgwick, Frank, *Ballads and Poems Illustrating English History*, Cambridge, 1907.

Stevens, G. A., *Songs Comic and Satyrical*, 1782.

Wilkins, W. W., *Political Ballads of the Seventeenth and Eighteenth Centuries*, 2 vols, 1860; reprinted 1968.

Williams, R. Vaughan, and Lloyd, A. L., *The Penguin Book of English Folk Songs*, 1959.

Zimmermann, G. D., *Songs of Irish Rebellion: Political Street Ballads and Rebel Songs, 1780–1900*, Dublin, 1967; reprinted Detroit, n.d.

GENERAL BACKGROUND

Aldis, H. G., 'Book production and distribution, 1625–1800', in *The Cambridge History of English Literature*, vol. XI, 1914.

Alnutt, W. H., 'Notes on the introduction of printing presses into the smaller towns of England and Wales, 1750–1800', *Library*, 2, 1901.

Ashton, J., *The Fleet: its River, Prison and Marriages*, 1888.

Blagden, C., 'Notes on the ballad market [in the seventeenth century]', in *Studies in Bibliography*, vi, 1954.

The Bloody Register: the Most Remarkable Trials, 1700–1764, 4 vols, 1764.

Bradfield, Nancy, *Historical Costumes of England, 1066–1968*, 3rd ed., 1970.

A Brief Description of the Cities of London and Westminster, 1776.

Burke, Thomas, *The Streets of London Through the Centuries*, 1940.

Chancellor, E. B., *The Eighteenth Century in London*, 1920.

Chandler, F. W., *The Literature of Roguery*, 2 vols, 1907, 1916.

Chappell, William, *Popular Music of the Olden Time*, 2 vols, 1853, 1859; reprinted as *Old English Popular Music*, ed. H. W. Woolridge, 2 vols in 1, New York, 1961.

Christie, W., and W. M., *Traditional Ballad Airs*, Edinburgh, 2 vols, 1876, 1881.

Dibdin, Charles, *A Collection of Songs*, new ed., 2 vols, 1814.

Dibdin, Charles, *The Musical Tour of Mr. Dibdin*, Sheffield, 1788.

Dibdin, Charles, *The Professional Life of Mr. Dibdin, written by himself*, 4 vols, 1803.

Dibdin, Charles, *Songs*, 2 vols, 1828, 1829.

Dibdin, Charles, see also entry under Kidson, Frank, below.

Dickens, Charles, *Sketches by 'Boz'*, 1836.

Folk-Song Journal, see below, *Journal of the English Folk Dance and Song Society* and *Journal of the English Folk-Song Society*.

Fowler, D. C., *A Literary History of the Popular Ballad*, Durham, North Carolina, 1968.

George, M. D., *London Life in the Eighteenth Century*, 1925; new ed., 1951.

George, M. D. (ed.), *England in Johnson's Day*, 1928.

Hindley, Charles, *The History of the Catnach Press*, 1886.

Hindley, Charles, *A History of the Cries of London*, 1881; 2nd ed., 1888.

Hindley, Charles, *The Life and Times of James Catnach*, 1878; reprinted Detroit, 1968.

Hone, William, *The Every-Day Book*, 2 vols, 1826–7.

Hughson, David, *A History and Description of London*, 4 vols, 1805–9.

Hughson, David, *Walks Through London*, 2 vols, 1817.

Journal of the English Folk Dance and Song Society, 1932—(successor to *Folk-Song Journal* and *Journal of the English Folk-Song Society*).

Journal of the English Folk-Song Society, 1899–1931.

Kelly, Francis, *A Short History of Costume and Armour*, 1931.

Kent, William (ed.), *An Encyclopaedia of London*, 1937; rev. ed., 1951.

Kidson, Frank, 'The ballad sheet and song garland', *Journal of the English Folk-Song Society*, no. VII, 1905.

Kidson, Frank, 'A Biography of Charles Dibdin', *Notes and Queries*, May 1907.

Kitchin, George, *A Survey of Burlesque and Parody in English*, Edinburgh, 1931.

Lloyd, A. L., *Folk Song in England*, 1967.

Lloyd, A. L., *The Singing Englishman: an Introduction to Folksong*, 1944.

Marks, A., *Tyburn Tree*, 1908.

The Microcosm of London, 3 vols, 1808; reprinted, 1904.

Mitchell, R. J., and Leys, M. D. R., *A History of London Life*, 1963.

Murray, T. A., *Remarks on the Situation of the Poor in the Metropolis*, 1801.

The Newgate Calendar, or, Malefactor's Bloody Register, c. 1774, 5 vols.

The New Newgate Calendar, c. 1826, 5 vols.

Pennant, Thomas, *Some Account of London*, 1790.

Plant, M., *The English Book Trade*, 1939; 2nd ed., 1965.

Plomer, H. R., *A Short History of English Printing 1476–1898*, 1900.

Plomer, H. R., *A Short History of English Printing 1476–1900*, 1915.

Previté-Orton, C. W., *Political Satire in English Poetry*, 1910; reprinted New York, 1969.

Routledge, James, *Chapters in the History of Popular Progress Chiefly in Relation to the Freedom of the Press and Trial by Jury, 1660–1820*, 1876.

Scott, G. R., *The History of Capital Punishment*, 1950.

Sharp, C. J., *English Folk Song: Some Conclusions*, 4th rev. ed., by M. Karpeles, 1965.

Shepard, Leslie, *The Broadside Ballad: a Study in Origins and Meanings*, 1962.

Shepard, Leslie, *John Pitts, Ballad Printer of Seven Dials, London, 1765–1844*, 1969.

Simpson, C. M., *The British Broadside Ballad and its Music*, New Brunswick, N.J., 1966.

Steinberg, S. H., *500 Years of Printing*, 1955.

Webb, R. K., *The British Working Class Reader, 1790–1848: Literacy and Social Tension*, 1955; reprinted New York, 1971.

Wells, E. K., *The Ballad Tree: a Study of British and American Ballads*, 1950.

Wimberly, L. C., *Folklore in the English and Scottish Ballads*, 1928; reprinted New York, 1959.

Wroth, W. and A. E., *The London Pleasure Gardens of the Eighteenth Century*, 1896.

GRAMOPHONE RECORDS

Ballads and Broadsides, sung by Louis Killen, Topic T126.

The Folk Songs of England, 10 vols, Topic Records.

Healy, J. N., *Songs of Cork and Kerry*, Mercier IRL 1.

The Long Harvest: Some Traditional Ballads in their English, Scots and North American Variants, sung by Peggy Seeger and Ewan MacColl, Argo, ZDA 66–75.

Morton, Robin, *Folksongs Sung in Ulster*, Mercier IRL 11.

Unto Brigg Fair: Joseph Taylor and other Traditional Lincolnshire Singers, recorded in 1908 by Percy Grainger, Leader Sound LEA 4050.

Index of Titles

References in parentheses are to volume and slip-sheet in the Madden Collection
Numbers refer to the order of ballads in this volume

Index of First Lines

Numbers refer to pages

294